THE JAPANESE NEGOTIATOR

THE JAPANESE NEGOTIATOR

Subtlety and Strategy Beyond Western Logic

Robert M. March

KODANSHA INTERNATIONAL
Tokyo and New York

Distributed in the United States by Kodansha International/ USA Ltd., 114 Fifth Avenue, New York, New York 10011. Published by Kodansha International Ltd., 17-14 Otowa 1-chome, Bunkyo-ku, Tokyo 112 and Kodansha International/USA Ltd.

First edition, 1989
Third printing, 1990

Library of Congress Cataloging-in-Publication Data
March, Robert M.
    The Japanese negotiator.

    Includes index.
    1. Negotiation in business—Japan.   2. National characteristics, Japanese.
HD58.6.M366   1988   658.4   88-80129
ISBN 0-87011-887-0 (U.S.)
ISBN 4-7700-1387-6 (Japan)

CONTENTS

Introduction   7

Part I. EFFECTIVE NEGOTIATION
        WITH THE JAPANESE   13

Chapter 1. Negotiations Among the Japanese   15

Everyday Japanese Negotiations   17
The Psychology of Japanese Negotiation   21
The Naniwabushi *Stategy   22*
Conclusion   32

Chapter 2. International Negotiation as
           a Well-Managed Process   34

Case Study: Setting Up a Joint Venture   36
Case Study: Negotiating an Overseas Mining Investment   43
Case Study: Accommodating Differences in Policy   47
Case Study: Nippon Texacom   51

Chapter 3. The Japanese Negotiating with Foreign Friends   56

Case Study: Two Broadcasting Organizations   57
Case Study: Negotiating with Your Kid Brother   60

Chapter 4. Managing Japanese Accounts   65

Case Study: The Importance of Knowing Japan   65
Case Study: A Professional American Negotiator   69
An Account Manager in Trouble   75
Conclusion   78

Part II. INEFFECTIVE NEGOTIATION
        WITH THE JAPANESE   81

Chapter 5. The Roots of Conflict   83

   Case Study: A Licensing Agreement Dispute 88
   Case Study: The Three-Billion-Dollar Sugar Dispute 97
   The Japanese Style of Conflict Escalation 107

Chapter 6. Japanese Attitudes Toward Contracts   111

   Lawyers 116
   The Betamax Lawsuit 119

Part III. TOWARD BETTER JAPANESE–WESTERN
         NEGOTIATION   125

Chapter 7. Typical Japanese Negotiation Strategies   127

   Normative Strategies 127
   Rational Strategies 131
   Assertive Strategies 138
   Avoidance Strategies 140
   Nonverbal Expression 141

Chapter 8. The Japanese Negotiator: An Assessment   153

   Japanese Strengths 153
   Japanese Weaknesses 155
   The Human Dimension 157

Chapter 9. Improving Japanese–Western Negotiation   161

   The Pre-Negotiation Stage 162
   The Opening Stage 164
   The Bargaining Stage 166
   The Complication Stage 167
   Resolving International Negotiation Problems 169
   The Four Stages of the Strategic Negotiation Process 172
   Using the Key Skills 177
   The Strategic Negotation Process: A Summary Statement 182

Bibliography   185

Index   193

INTRODUCTION

Every negotiator faces the same vexing question: How can I figure out what the person on the other side really thinks and wants, and what is the real meaning of his words and actions? If you and your opponent share a common language and culture, you can often fall back on insight and intuition. But these may serve no purpose when you face someone whose language and culture are a mystery to you, whose categories of thought, values, and perceptions are rooted in historical, religious, and social circumstances that are alien to your own. For most of us, the Japanese are such a people.

This book stems from a conviction that when we really understand what the other person is thinking and seeking, and what his words and actions really mean, cross-cultural negotiations will become smoother and international goodwill will be fostered. For some ten years, this conviction has motivated me to improve the negotiating skills of international businessmen. Most importantly, in executive training programs in Japan and elsewhere, I have pitted Japanese and Western participants against one another in negotiation role plays, with both sides continuously observed by both video cameras and people. When the role plays are finished, all the data—observers' reports, video tapes, observations of the players, and my own comments—are presented in a thorough analysis, evaluation, and review. Both individuals and teams have their performances evaluated (usually for the first time in their lives), their weaknesses and strengths highlighted. Yet even more important than this, the participants say, are the insights they gain into how the other side thinks and reacts, especially during recesses when they discuss as though in private the problems that have emerged.

I have used this technique for many years in business negotiation courses in Japan that are attended by both American and Japanese graduate students. At our first class meeting, without any introduction to the subject, I often split the class into an American negotiating team, a Japanese negotiating team, and a mixed group of observers and monitors. I then give each team very different instructions for negotiating, for instance, how class grades will be calculated. The Japanese must argue for grades based 100 percent on work assignments, while the Americans must insist on a 50 percent grade for participation in class discussions.

Each team, along with observers, retires to a separate room to prepare for the negotiating session. Thirty minutes later, the session begins and runs for about an hour and a half. Observers, by means of a standard form, record details of the teams' behavior and their interpersonal dynamics throughout the negotiation. Then we analyze what has happened. Invariably, the experiences and lessons drawn from the exercise are similar every year. In addition, they are strikingly like real-life Japanese–American business negotiations.

A summary of the reports of observers for a typical year notes that, in preparing for negotiations, the Japanese will develop defensive arguments with no consideration of persuading, selling, or converting the other side. They do not consider what the other side might be thinking or offering, or try to foresee its strategies. Nor do they consider concession options. A strong consensus is reached based on the arguments supporting their position after the leader has reviewed the arguments and everyone has jotted them down. There is strong group cohesion.

In the actual negotiations, the Japanese side gives the "appearance of being somewhat overwhelmed by the Americans, although it did not in fact make as many concessions." The tone of the negotiation "seemed to indicate that the Americans were dominating, when in fact the Japanese were only being out-talked, not out-negotiated."

The Japanese typically show little physical or verbal activity, but they nod frequently, suggesting to Western observers, and to the American team, that their minds are being changed. An aggressive approach easily pushes them into a defensive position, and they become less willing to yield.

The observers also point out the following Japanese characteristics in negotiation: the Japanese are frustrated by the difficulties of negotiating in English, where their skills are imperfect; they have problems in conveying what they mean in English; they are unwilling either to form a consensus or to express disagreement in front of their opponents; they give strong nonverbal support to their leaders; and their final counteroffers are often innovative, offering benefits to both sides.

As for the American team's preparation for negotiations, observers stated that they (unlike the Japanese) will take time to try and predict how the other side will conduct the negotiations. In the actual negotiation, they decide to explore the other side's approach and then go on the offensive. They agree to ask initially for more than they want and to take a low-keyed approach. In reality, however, they are not low-keyed but are concerned with proving that their position is right in order to convert the Japanese to their viewpoint. Americans show a stronger and more explicit desire to win, emphasize the benefits to the other party, and make passionate presentations with the goal of winning, in contrast to the Japanese goal of defending their position. Observers repeatedly describe the American negotiating style as highly aggressive. But Americans only appear to dominate as they keep agreeing with each other and disagreeing with the other side.

Observers with international business experience often note that such role plays correspond closely to actual business negotiations. One writes, "The American team bombarded the Japanese side with ideas and the use of logic, while the Japanese side lent a seemingly attentive ear and made no specific commitments." Role plays also reveal how a negotiation style that is effective at home can be ineffective and inappropriate "abroad." They reveal how difficult it is to "read" the real intentions or thoughts of the other side, an aspect that recurs frequently in the case studies that make up much of this book.

In what way can a book match actual experience, analyzed and reflected upon? I have tried to make it mirror as closely as possible the actual experience of negotiating with the Japanese. I hope it provides a unique spyhole on the hidden dynamics and hidden roots of the Japanese negotiating style. It will show what the Japanese discuss in private, what they emphasize or neglect, how they size others up, their strategies and tactics. This will be shown mostly through actual case studies, where I have been able to present what really happened on both sides. Most of the cases are noteworthy, some are "sensational." All, I consider, can be identified with.

I have tried not to write a negotiation "cookbook," to be read in one sitting on the plane to Tokyo (though it might be). I have tried not to oversimplify either the cases or the interpretations. Understanding others is as time-consuming as understanding oneself. There are many quick tips to be picked up, but the book will work best if you immerse yourself mentally in the cases, and let them percolate in your mind. However, in focusing mainly on the Japanese, the book provides an incomplete picture of the critical factors in negotiations: in particular, *you* are missing. You—the non-Japanese, with your skills and behavior patterns, your personal appeal, your quirks and blind spots—may have a more decisive impact on the outcome of the negotiation than any differences in objectives or any failures in communication. A negotiator should be chosen with the utmost care, as many of the cases reveal. In this way, increased self-understanding might be another reward of reflecting on what is written here.

An important objective of this book is to prepare you to analyze and cope with situations of misunderstanding, difficulty, or conflict in negotiations with the Japanese. But to say this is to suggest that difficulties *always* arise, which is not true. In my experiences in Japan over a long period, I have found there may be fewer difficulties than in the West. There may be times when negotiations go so smoothly that you have to conclude that they must, after all, be culture-free. Treasure the thought, for it is altogether too easy in Japan to find that one has inadvertently said or done the wrong thing and made an enemy or lost a friend or client—for the Japanese are a proud and particular and exclusive-minded people.

The main focus of the book is on understanding Japanese business negotiation style in relation to Western business people. For this reason, the first chapter is devoted to explaining how the Japanese negotiate at home with other Japanese. Since they, just as anyone else, will come into an international negotiation using their own home style, it is critical for those of us who would negotiate with them to understand exactly what that is.

The following four chapters deal with actual cases of international negotiations. In Chapters 2, 3, and 4, I deal with negotiations that were well managed and, despite conflicts and misunderstandings along the way, had successful outcomes. These include, in Chapter 2, setting up joint ventures, making overseas investments, and negotiations on policy differences; in Chapter 3, effective negotiations between related companies are shown; in Chapter 4, negotiations involved in maintaining ongoing relationships (which we will call "account management") are dealt with.

Chapter 5 presents cases that were less effectively managed, more acrimonious, hostile, and conflict-ridden. In demonstrating how deep the roots of conflict can go in Japanese–Western negotiations, these provide the most valuable lessons for anyone who will be negotiating with the Japanese.

Chapter 6 deals with an issue of particular concern to Americans, the lack among the Japanese of a strong legalistic sense, and how this affects their attitude to contracts. This major source of conflict and misunderstanding is unlikely to change suddenly in the near future.

Chapters 7 and 8 provide answers to general questions, such as what strategies and tactics the Japanese most often adopt in their dealings with Westerners. Chapter 7 examines the cases presented earlier, among other material, to make a full accounting of the Japanese negotiating style. In Chapter 8, I present a view of the Japanese negotiator as a human being, with his strengths and failings, to allow greater understanding and empathy.

The final chapter is based on a systematic model of international negotiation, and presents a negotiation management process—termed the Strategic Negotiation Process (SNP)—with the aim of making cross-cultural negotiations less conflict-ridden and more effective for both parties.

Finally, I should mention that in order to protect confidentiality, in almost all cases I have changed company and personal names.

Part

I

EFFECTIVE NEGOTIATION
WITH
THE JAPANESE

Chapter *1*

Negotiations Among the Japanese

Among themselves, the truth is that the Japanese do not like negotiation. It has disagreeable connotations of confrontation, to be avoided whenever possible. The Japanese instinct is for agreements worked out behind the scenes, on the basis of give and take, harmony and long-term interest. In fact, except for a handful with extensive international experience, very few Japanese even know how to negotiate in the Western sense. In everyday life in Japan, there is little experience of bargaining to buy household goods at lower prices, or even of using arguments in a debating fashion to win points. The common Western ideal of a persuasive communicator—one who is highly skilled in argumentation, who overcomes objections with verbal flair, who is an energetic extrovert—would be regarded by most Japanese as superficial, insincere, and, more subtly, a little vulgar. What the Japanese learn in their culture is that vagueness in discussion is a virtue. They learn to involve others, to listen to their views, and, when no strongly dissenting views remain, a decision is made. It is noteworthy that nobody seems to make the actual decision, rather it just seems to "happen." As for individual involvement as a Japanese, everyone knows that as long as you remain silent, you project a favorable impression and are assumed to be thinking deeply about the problem. Of course, you may have other reasons for keeping quiet: you may, for instance, simply have nothing to say; you may be a poor talker; the subject may be a painful one to you; or—and this is very common—others may have put matters so clearly that the best you can do is keep quiet. Finally, even if you do speak up, it will be usual for you to speak ambiguously (an elegant Japanese way of describing this is "*Tamamushi-iro no hyōgen o tsukau,*" "Using iridescent expressions").

The culturally approved use of ambiguity in Japan extends even to the business setting, where it is linked in the Japanese mind to the issue of personal trust. Whereas foreign—especially American—negotiators may develop bargaining ranges and strategic options as a matter of course in their pre-negotiation planning, this is still rare among the Japanese. This is especially true when the foreigner adopts a bargaining, or a "horse trading," approach. One or two counterproposals may be in order, but an invitation to "horse trade" provokes in many Japanese a certain aristocratic disdain for the merchant mind. This disdain may become extreme when the Japanese negotiate among themselves, for there is a widespread view that if you are an Oriental you will not promote your own ideas. Rather, it is up to others to recognize your merits. An Oriental gentleman should sit impassively and with Confucian detachment before others, never appearing to be a merchant. An Oriental gentleman influences others, especially his subordinates, by subtle, indirect suggestion, relying upon their thorough indoctrination in the hierarchical society to ensure that orders are carried out faithfully. If the necessity arises, a middleman may speak on one's behalf. When circumstances become unbearable, then an appeal of melodramatic pathos is perfectly in order, for that is not considered negotiation but an appeal to the heart that transcends crude, rational considerations.

The irony of the preceding paragraph may be somewhat

heavy, but it is still commonly accepted that if two parties trust each other, money and other details need not be discussed. Thus, in many industries in Japan neither contracts nor invoices nor even product catalogs are used. On occasions when contracts are used, a point will be made of not reading the fine print, for to do so would imply a lack of trust. These residual aristocratic values are also behind the absence of prices on menus in many high-class Japanese restaurants and bars, or on products sold in traditional shops.

Despite this, the Japanese employ an array of means to influence others and achieve their goals, means that, if not completely unknown in the West, are often carried to extremes that seem bizarre or undignified to Westerners. The reason behind such behavior is that they are doing everything they can to avoid appearing either self-centered (as they fear they would were they to speak about the merits or superiority of their company or their products) or coldly rational (as they also fear they would were they to concentrate only on economic or business issues, without relating sympathetically to the other side). There are powerful injunctions in Japanese society against both of these attitudes, and their behavior will make better sense if this is understood. The fact that one can also meet Japanese businessmen who are manifestly self-centered and cold "economic animals" is, in my view, only to encounter exceptions to a still valid generalization.

EVERYDAY JAPANESE NEGOTIATIONS

The following short summaries present behavioral patterns that are typical of the relationship between Japanese buyers and sellers.

Patience Pays Off: Saburo Matsuo is a salesman with a major securities company. As a result of a tip, he learned that one of Japan's richest and most famous men was beginning to dabble in the stock market. The approach he decided on was this: he would stand outside the rich man's house every morning and bow to him as he left for the office. For three months, six mornings a week, he kept this up, and finally the great man began to acknowledge his bow. He continued for another three months, even though he had no chance to talk to his prospective client. Finally, one morning, Matsuo, in his customary place, was caught in a heavy downpour without an umbrella. As the famous man's car pulled out, Matsuo was standing in the rain, bowing as usual. The car came to a halt and the door opened. "Get in!" the famous man ordered. Matsuo got in. That was the beginning of a discussion about the stock market and the acquisition of a new client for Matsuo's company. What Matsuo's conduct over the six-month period demonstrated (in terms of Japanese cultural values) was that Matsuo was sincerely interested in serving his clients, not in bragging about his own products or services.

Extracurricular Service: Shoji Meguro is a sales supervisor for a large food company in a rural town north of Tokyo, with his particular responsibility being frozen foods. A dedicated man, he usually works six and a half days a week, including Sundays, the busiest day for supermarkets, which are his principal customers. However, his service to his supermarket clients does not stop with frozen foods. In his region, supermarkets are renovated and redesigned at frequent intervals. As a matter of course, he helps by donating actual physical labor, working from morning to night to get the remodeled store ready for customers.

Does he do this reluctantly? Are there subtle social pressures obliging him to perform these seemingly extraneous activities? Not at all. As he sees it, "It is only in such situations that I can develop a natural relationship with my customers. Customers who are ordinarily tight-lipped loosen up in these conditions, and I can get to hear what they really think about things."

Personal Relationships First: Yoshiko Nakai is a senior saleswoman for a bed manufacturer and has been representing the company in the Tokyo–Yokohama region for fifteen years. She has long recognized that selling to Japanese housewives is impossible if she takes a mercenary attitude, with a view only to making a sale. Whenever she receives an inquiry, even if she is sure that it is unlikely to result in a sale, she follows it up. She gives top priority to personal relationships. For instance, from time to time she calls on old customers to find that their husbands have recently passed away. A wife and mother herself, she responds immediately to the situation; she takes the new widow's hands and they cry freely together. Mrs. Nakai is one of her company's leading salespeople.

"Never Mention Your Product": A few years ago I had the opportunity to observe a most unusual (to foreigners) form of Japanese "negotiation" when I accompanied a pharmaceutical drug salesman on his daily rounds. These salesmen are known as *"puropa"* in the drug industry, a word derived from the English word "propaganda."

The day began with an 8:30 A.M. appointment at a drug wholesaler, with whom this *puropa*—let us call him Shinji Suzuki—works. He gave a ten-minute lecture to the wholesaler's staff on the clinical evidence for a new drug. The salesmen were attentive and asked several questions. Suzuki, a graduate pharmacist from a major Japanese university, handled them pleasantly and professionally. Although he enjoyed this experience, the rest of the day was to be less enjoyable.

After visiting a second wholesaler, where he talked to individual salesmen, we made our first visit to a general practitioner, entering the doctor's crowded waiting room at 10 A.M.

"How can you get through to the doctor?" I asked.

"Normally it's difficult," he replied. "The best time is what we call the 'golden time,' between noon and 2 P.M. However, right now I am going to see if he wants me to take his wife shopping."

I looked at him incredulously.

"Yes, as a matter of fact I take three wives shopping, and two days a week I pick up one doctor's children from kindergarten and take them home."

It was still too early to call on other physicians, so Suzuki invited me to a coffee shop. Clearly, he was well known there. We sat and made small talk, and smoked until the ashtray overflowed. I became nervous about this wasted time.

At 11:50, we made our next call on a general practitioner. Tired and irritable, perhaps from his morning's work, the doctor spoke brusquely and arrogantly to Suzuki: "I'm not interested in hearing about your company's new drugs, Suzuki. How many times have I told you that?"

Suzuki replied submissively, but good-naturedly, "Many times," then switched the conversation to golf. Had the doctor tried out the new putter he bought? Was he able to get away to the local medical association tournament last week? The doctor relaxed and spoke freely about golf. He finally terminated the call with, "I'm off to lunch now. Look in and see if my wife wants anything."

When we returned to the car, I expressed surprise at the extent of the doctor's arrogance. "How do you remain so composed at those times?" I queried.

"I am never completely composed at any time," he said in a measured way, "but I understand how he feels. Each month he may have as many as a hundred *puropa* calling on him. They all have the same story to tell, and he has heard it all before. What doctors like him really want is a service and friendship relationship, in return for which he buys our products. That's his policy: 'If you never mention your product, I'll buy it.'"

He continued, "Instead of talking about the product, we give service, such as by taking members of his family here and there, and we give friendship by playing golf with him, and even by drinking together occasionally. If I was to talk product to him, he would just see me as a low-class peddler, and no relationship would be possible. I accept that the doctor's social status is substantially higher than mine, and that helps him to feel comfortable with me."

THE PSYCHOLOGY OF JAPANESE NEGOTIATION

Japanese-style negotiation and customer service reflect those deep-seated values and customs inherent in the culture. Every culture, of course, has two sides: an ideological side that comprises a utopian version of the culture and its highest ideals; and a side that reflects how things really are. The ideological side of Japanese culture emphasizes service and doing favors and small kindnesses, stresses goodness and virtue as models to follow, and values indirect suggestion and intuitive knowledge of things. In reality, however, Japan is a society where, compared to the West, the exercise of power plays a great part in influencing behavior, while persuasive argumentation is less important. Powerful people command and exercise influence because the consequences of failing to do what a powerful person requires are feared as being devastating, even to the point of resulting in the loss of one's social status and social acceptance, and perhaps even of one's livelihood.

It is generally true that "wise hawks" (i.e., stronger parties) in Japan conceal, deftly and elegantly, their "talons" (so goes a famous proverb, "*Nō aru take wa tsume o kakusu*"), but it is rare for anyone to be in doubt as to what the relative power of each party is. Moreover, talons are likely to be revealed if the other party persists in disagreeing or, instead of simply complying with the more powerful party's proposal, tries to resort to a more rational approach to the resolution of a problem. Parties with influence are not regarded as independent elements in society; rather, they behave as though they are interdependent within a hierarchical society, where one is, and acts like, a boss, and it is definitely not advisable to argue with someone who is a boss. This perfectly mirrors the reality found within a

Japanese organization that every company employee knows but which, nevertheless, shocks Westerners when they discover it. As a Japanese, you don't argue with your boss if you want to succeed in the organization.

THE *NANIWABUSHI* STRATEGY

If you ask Japanese businessmen to describe the most typical Japanese method of resolving or avoiding disputes, they will most frequently answer *"naniwabushi."* These are popular Japanese ballads dating back to the Edo period (1600–1868), whose performers chant tales of chivalrous robbers and the rise and fall of great families. There are three parts to a ballad: the opening, or *kikkake*, which gives the general background of the story and tells what the people involved are thinking or feeling; the *seme*, or a narrative of critical events; and the final *urei*, which expresses pathos and sorrow at what has happened.

In business, a negotiation following the *naniwabushi* structure might go as follows. Suppose you wish to negotiate revised terms of payment for your automobile because of a business recession. In your approach to the finance company, you open with a statement that describes your relationship with them over the years. You tell them what a good customer you have been, how meticulous you have been about making payments on time, how you have brought new customers to them, and so on. This is the *kikkake*.

In the *seme*, you focus on the disastrous effects the recession has had on your business. Turnover has declined, you have severely pruned costs, your family now eats nothing but (the Japanese equivalent of) Big Macs, you've given up this and that, but it is still not enough. You can only continue to survive if the payments are cut in half.

In the *urei*, you explain what will happen to you if the creditors do not grant this request. You will lose the automobile and thereby all your income. Then you will not be able to pay them anything! So you plead, "Grant my request," implying that if they do not and something untoward happens to you, it will be their fault entirely.

Thus, *naniwabushi* begins with a recounting of the background, which is followed by a dramatic account of the crisis, and concludes with an anguished plea for leniency, embroidered with the dire consequences should the request be denied. A *naniwabushi* plea can be dressed up appealingly with melodrama. For example, you can take your starving wife and children with you and have them stand silently, weeping at your side; or you might indicate how close you are to self-destruction by producing a pistol or sword or bottle of poison at the right psychological moment.

Naniwabushi is artful, premeditated, calculated—and in Japan it works. The more tragic and moving the story, the easier it is for Japanese listeners to forget contracts or commitments. Indeed, listeners who do not compromise or show compassion in such circumstances would be condemned as being cold-hearted or mercenary.

Robert Klineberg, an American businessman in Tokyo, was able to use a modified *naniwabushi* most effectively with his realtor. He lives in an elegant old house in the ancient city of Kamakura, south of Tokyo. The house, owned by a Japanese ambassador to Europe, is close to the beach, surrounded by lofty pine trees, romantic in style, with a moderate rent. The sole problem was that the roof leaked, seriously and often. When Klineberg first moved in, he had asked for the ceiling and roof to be repaired, and the realtor had promised to do everything he could to make him comfortable. But when a sudden typhoon dumped water onto his piano and stereo, he asked for urgent action. However, only the ceiling was repaired, with nothing but promises about the roof, leaving him more and more distressed by his physical environment, but uncertain as to how to get the realtor to act. The following week, he and I discussed the problem, and I suggested that he tackle the problem in a more Japanese way, as follows: first, behaving in a dignified, proud, but stern manner, he should review the relationship between them, the promises made, how he had always been a model tenant, paid his rent on time, and so on. This is the *kikkake*. Second, his *seme* should proceed truthfully "but, the house has become difficult to live in, it is damp, summer will be with us soon and that means mildew everywhere, I can't entertain friends here any more, my life is becoming intolerable." The *seme* demands exaggerated but clear expression of pain and sadness, with a hint of restrained anger.

Klineberg considered my suggestions, met with the realtor, and acted out his *naniwabushi* with melodramatic aplomb. He began sternly, refused the seat offered him, objected to the realtor bringing other staff members into the negotiation (they were sent out again), hit hard on his inability to entertain, and was able to mix anger, sadness, and disbelief nicely in his final *urei*, when he faced the realtor, and, simultaneously, slammed his hand down on a steel file, looked tearful, and cried out, "Are you a man of your word?" The realtor looked aghast, and kept saying in an agonized voice *"Komatta! Komatta!"* (meaning roughly "This is terrible!"). In the final negotiation, Klineberg held out for, and was able to obtain, agreement to all of his demands in line with the realtor's original general promise.

Klineberg's experience is but one of many that show the Japanese susceptibility to sad stories. A clue lies in the melodramatic quality of *naniwabushi* and permissive Japanese attitudes to self-pity. With little exaggeration, it may be said that every Japanese, in his heart, is the hero of a great melodrama starring himself. It is a drama of each man's heroic struggle to achieve modest success in the face of society's adamantine rules and the keen competition of other men. At the same time, however, the Japanese, as hero, sees others suffering the same difficulties as himself and thus responds compassionately, as a man of honor.

This melodramatic bias appears not only in domestic *naniwabushi*-type negotiations but also in international negotiations, for example, in the sugar dispute presented in Chapter 4. The American political scientist Michael Blaker (1977) has written about Japan's international diplomatic negotiating style, pointing out the florid language and anguished pleas used by Japanese diplomats and politicians in the last-ditch stages of negotiations. Phrases like the following are common: "We must endure the unendurable." "It must be war or undeserved hardship." "We no longer have room to move." They assert that "great efforts" or "great sacrifices" have been made or that "the uncompromisable has been compromised," albeit in vain. But such rationalizations serve to clear the consciences of all involved.

Japanese negotiators, when faced with failure, seek to shift the blame onto someone else. Blaker comments that "beneath attempts to transfer the blame is the belief that Japanese policies are intrinsically correct." Until failure is conceded, the Japanese persistently believe that if only the right method can be discovered—for instance, the right negotiator or the right communication style, whether man-to-man discussion or a frank exchange of views—then a breakthrough is possible.

Blaker's research shows that the Japanese negotiator, as hero, is a character of melodrama, and that Japanese national psychology contains a strong vein of conscious innocence. The Japanese appear to be saying to themselves, "Whatever harm happens to me, as the hero of my own melodrama, is unearned and undeserved. I am a victim of blind fate." To believe that one is right, and to experience no uncertainty about that rightness, is vintage melodrama.

Keigo Okonogi, a leading Japanese psychiatrist, explains how this unique Japanese psychology works, and warns the Japanese of their tendency:

Japanese psychology is so structured that people can only

admit their own aggression by placing those who attack them in the position of powerful and unfair assailants and by casting themselves as weak victims whether or not it is actually the case; subjectively they always set a limit to their patience and endurance. A classic example is the imperial proclamation of the opening of hostilities in the Pacific War and the attack on Pearl Harbor, made to settle old scores with "fiendish America and Britain." We should be on our guard against the tendency, occasionally seen even today, to perceive international problems in terms of this traditional psychological context. (*The Japan Echo* VI, no. 1 [1979], p. 113.)

In other words, when the Japanese are threatened or attacked by others, they see it immediately as unfair. They see themselves as weak, defenseless, and victimized, thus requiring from the attacker some explicit compensation—at least a sincere apology or, in serious cases, the tangible tribute of consolation money.

This victim mentality (*higaisha ishiki*) appears frequently in both domestic and international business negotiations. In the Japan–Australia sugar dispute dealt with in Chapter 4, the Japanese sugar refineries felt deeply victimized by events that led to the sharp drop in world sugar prices and local demand. In 1987, when the yen strengthened drastically against the dollar, most Japanese commentators complained about the unfairness to Japan, and could not grasp that the biggest foreign concern was about rising unemployment and declining industrial competitiveness in the face of Japanese competitive strength. The Japanese could only see that the strong yen was hurting their export business, which was making *them* victims.

The *naniwabushi* discussion should alert you to the fact that many of the Japanese you face do not think about problems in the way you do. By the end of the book this is going to be one of the major lessons to be drawn. When things go smoothly for the Japanese, they will be more rational than you. When things don't go smoothly, rationality may go out the window. Be prepared! Here are some other ways in which the Japanese influence or are influenced by others.

Conscience: In Japan, the influence of personal conscience or moral sense on the behavior of an individual is powerful. A common saying, abjuring one from behaving improperly is: "Even if others do not know, Heaven knows, Earth knows, and I know." The Japanese see themselves as *ryōshinteki na minzoku* (conscience-motivated people), and appeals to the conscience of individuals can be highly effective among the Japanese, simplifying the process of negotiation. If the police exhort the criminal to "be a man," or challenge him with "you're a human being, aren't you? So tell the truth," this may be all that is necessary to secure a confession. The Japanese realtor showed exactly this in his reaction to Klineberg's "Are you a man of your word?"

"Nemawashi": This is the practice of preliminary and informal sounding out of people's ideas about a project or a course of action before a formal proposal is drawn up. It is, one can say, standard procedure for the Japanese in both their personal and business life. *Nemawashi* originally meant the binding up of the roots of a tree prior to its being transplanted, and this implication of preparation is important when *nemawashi* is undertaken within a company. If people have strong objections to a proposal, or new ideas to improve a proposal, *nemawashi* enables these to be discovered in advance, making the acceptance of the final, formal proposal more certain.

Pre-giving: Japan's society is extremely stable and its members have little mobility, often living in the same town and working for the same company all their adult lives. Thus, their lives are highly predictable, and they know in real terms what their wealth and income will be in, say, ten or twenty years, and to a certain extent what their circle of acquaintances will be. Such an atmosphere encourages the strategy of pre-giving, which means rewarding someone before they comply with a request. A common example is the giving of gifts on first meeting certain people (such as teachers and politicians) from whom one hopes later to receive favors. Pre-giving may be thought of as a key strategy of child socialization, and of bonding adults to organizations. It creates feelings of indebtedness, and a readiness to repay on demand.

Debt: Every Japanese, it has been said, has a ledger inside his head, into which he enters every instance of pre-giving, that is, every favor received and every favor given. The ledger also reflects the personal connections, or *kone*, that individual Japanese have and like to boast of when something has to be investigated or accomplished. Such connections are usually those who owe a favor, so one is in a good position to get something done, without having to negotiate for it. The negotiation, as it were, has already been completed.

Note, however, what the psychiatrist Okonogi (1977) has to say about the subtleties of Japanese debt and pre-giving.

> The Japanese method of adaptation [to others] eschews the assertion of individual rights and ignores the principle of give-and-take, instead evoking a sense of. . . guilt at not having repaid the debt. Appealing to this sense of guilt prompts obedience. . . .
>
> If the benefactor [the giver or pre-giver]. . . does not demand gratitude or accept repayment, the gratitude of the beneficiary becomes *on* (obligation). The benefactor who demands repayment is criticized as a small-minded person who dwells on favors done and obligations due. Conversely, the voluntary repayment of an obligation when a natural occasion arises is regarded as one of the most moving virtues.

In other words, debt and pre-giving only become meaningful if one is part of the Japanese social system and can demonstrate one's sincerity and humanity by unanticipated, natural repayments of debt to one's benefactors. In spite of Okonogi's denial of the principle of give-and-take, the "you scratch my back and I'll scratch yours" attitude of calculated debt and pre-giving is not entirely absent from Japanese business.

Advice: Giving advice is customary. In Japan, human relationships are often dictated by the powerful *"sempai–kohai"* (elder–younger) relationship. Seniors are expected to give advice to juniors, and juniors treat it much more seriously than in the West.

Ostracism: In Japan, the threat of ostracism—that is, ceasing contact and communication with someone, or excluding them from their primary support group—is probably the key technique of social control and influence. The Japanese who refuses to accept a proposal or request that everyone else in the group accepts is likely to be threatened with ostracism. "If you don't agree to our proposal, we'll tell everyone what a rascal you've been, and nobody will do business with you any more" goes the thinking. In fact, there is an element of bullying in Japanese-style threats, and ostracism is the inevitable outcome if the other party refuses to come to terms. This is the most feared outcome in a tight-knit society such as Japan.

In any discussion of the Japanese businessman's ideas about business strategy and negotiation, it is useful to look at an Oriental philosophy of behavior, that of the noted Chinese military strategist Sun-tzu (Sonshi in Japanese). Sun-tzu lived during the early fourth century B.C., but his ideas still prevail in Japan today and are much in evidence in books and magazine articles. A stickler for discipline, Sun-tzu continues to point the way for leaders in business and government, and his ideas are consonant with deep currents in Japanese culture.

The following are some of his most important axioms (taken from a recent Japanese translation of and essay on his "Art of War").

"To defeat the enemy psychologically is the superior strategy. To defeat the enemy militarily is the inferior strategy."

"The warrior's way is one of deception. The key to success is to capitalize upon your power to do the unexpected, when appearing to be unprepared."

The key to understanding Sun-tzu's approach and philosophy lies in these axioms. They are knowledge of one's own resources and capabilities, intelligence about the field of battle and the enemy's strength, patience, and whatever dissembling is necessary to deceive and catch the enemy off-guard.

For modern Japanese businessmen, these lessons continue to be valued. Patient intelligence work—collecting information without giving anything away—is a key to the strength of Japanese business. Information-gathering is institutionalized within Japanese culture and Japanese business. Junior employees as a matter of course write reports about their external activities, training programs, trips, and meetings. Unlike Westerners, the Japanese do not question or pass judgment on the usefulness of this information. Grass-roots intelligence work involving the input of many people is used to create a mosaic picture, and they proceed with caution, hesitating to draw any early conclusions. Many Westerners have probably noticed how almost compulsively curious the Japanese are for all kinds of information. What they may not have realized is that, from a corporate view, this curiosity amounts to tactical intelligence work.

Industrial espionage (*sangyō supai* or *kigyō supai*) is a pejorative term in Japan. Nobody wants to talk about it, and to mention it is subtly insulting. While researching this topic, I tried to find individuals who might know something about the field, but I was indirectly warned that this was not a topic to be discussed publicly. Some Japanese told me that the seniority system in Japanese organizations is actually a deterrent to industrial espionage, since the older men are more prudent and cautious than their subordinates. Moreover, I was told, some older men have also been influenced by the wartime nationalistic doctrine of *"shinshū fumetsu ron,"* or "the theory of the immortality of the state (or organization)," which implies an innate superiority, and thus makes spying unnecessary.

There have been cases over the years of Japanese industrial espionage. In 1983, in the United States, IBM sued several companies for stealing computer secrets. In 1984, officials of the Ministry of Health and Welfare were arrested for selling drug formulae to Japanese pharmaceutical companies. Another case involved two textile companies, which subsequently had a major impact on the sales of paper shredders. To Sun-tzu the role of the intelligence gatherer was an honorable one because information is the key to his concept of warfare (*"Hei wa kidō nari,"* that is, "Deception is the way of the warrior").

While most Japanese businessmen would be ashamed to be spies or hire spies, patent dissembling and the disguising of real feelings or true intentions are very central to Japanese and Chinese culture. Humility, self-effacement, and the absence of pretension are cultivated social virtues. In business negotiations, the Japanese often use a tactic of concealing the top man, who positions himself on the fringe of his company's team, looking inconspicuous and initially making no contribution, while someone much his junior acts as spokesman.

Another aspect of the Japanese negotiating style is the sounding out of the other side about what it wants before making an offer, a variant of *nemawashi*, discussed earlier. This lends a vagueness to the early stages of Japanese negotiating activity that often smacks of furtiveness to foreigners. To the Japanese, however, it is the only sensible (Sun-tzu-like) way to know the other side. From the viewpoint of Japanese cultural wisdom, it is folly to make offers or proposals until you know what the other side wants. In this respect, the slow Japanese start-up, the absence of initial proposals, and the sounding out of the other side, along with the long drawn-out preliminary groundwork on their own side, mean that the Japanese are likely to enter a negotiation much more prepared than non-Japanese.

CONCLUSION

We have seen that the salient aspects of Japanese domestic negotiation style are intuition, indirectness, disguising or suppressing real feelings, persistence, avoidance of self-praise (where self includes one's company or products), patient dissembling, and diligent information-gathering about the other sides' needs or intentions. In crisis situations, the use of a melodramatic *naniwabushi*-like appeal is still common within Japan, though more calculated in its use than a generation ago.

Verbal contracts remain widespread because Japanese men continue to value their public reputations (their "face") as men of honor, and this sense of honor, as we will see, can make them especially sensitive, even overly so, to suggestions that they are not to be trusted or that they are unfair, or, in some contexts, unsportsmanlike.

From a Western viewpoint, much of the Japanese domestic negotiation style looks merely perverse. Obliqueness, avoidance, disdain for frankness, a refined tendency to call things by other names seem mere contrariness for its own sake—as though the individual is thinking, "No one is going to get me to do anything as conventional as calling a spade a spade." Such perversity is not uncommon among members of Japan's high business echelons, as the Warner–Natsuyama case (Chapter 4) or Nippon Texacom case (Chapter 2) indicate.

Western businessmen need to understand the Japanese domestic negotiation style. While it is true that you will often deal with highly Westernized Japanese, whose style is not dissimilar to your own, it is equally likely that you will encounter businessmen whose values and ways of doing business are vastly different.

Of course, even Japanese businessmen without any international experience recognize the fact that Westerners are different, that we are less predictable for them, that we think about many issues differently. But mere recognition of differences need be no basis for understanding or tolerance when conflicts of interest occur. It is one purpose of this book, by showing cases of difficulties in negotiations, to suggest ways in which Japanese and Westerners can negotiate more effectively with each other.

Chapter 2

International Negotiation as a Well-Managed Process

Few human activities are more fascinating to the layman than negotiation, but opinions as to what negotiation really is vary greatly. Some think of it as somewhat like a game of tennis or pingpong. You make an offer, your opponent makes a counteroffer, then the action moves to and fro until one side or the other wins the point. Each side feels it is negotiating according to the same set of rules, and both sides share a sense of fair play. They can see, as it were, what the opponent is doing, so information other than that gained in the flow of play is of little use.

Others see negotiation as purely tactical, full of subtlety, shrewd, and merciless. In this, while the skills of each player are important, there is no defined playing area, no mutually agreed upon rules, perhaps not even a sense of fair play. If negotiation in the first view is like tennis, in this other view it is more like two hunters stalking each other, and it can easily degenerate into something like hit-and-run guerrilla warfare.

The game-type and the tactical-type may be viewed as the two extremes of negotiation. If, for example, a difference arises between a Japanese supplier and his long-time Japanese client, since they both want the relationship to continue, their negotiation is likely to be friendly, cooperative, gamelike, and quick to come to a resolution. On the other hand, if a commodity buyer is visiting a foreign country to make a once-off purchase from foreigners he has never dealt with before and may never deal with again, he is likely to have reservations about trusting the foreigners, to have a different concept of what is fair, not to mention different price and delivery requirements. The strangeness of the situation and the lack of previous contact will make for a high-risk situation, and many negotiators will opt for a more cautious, personally distant, distrustful, and close-to-the-chest approach that is preeminently tactical.

Generally speaking, the game-type negotiation approximates domestic (i.e., Japanese versus Japanese) situations where the protagonists are known to one another or are mutually dependent upon the same social system and business values. Of course, the competitive element remains dominant (otherwise it would not be a game), but cooperation is also fostered through shared, familiar values. Although these values differ between cultures, businessmen of every culture readily recognize the need to play the game of negotiation at home according to the rules.

The tactical type of negotiation occurs more frequently in the international area simply because familiarity is absent and shared values are few. Still, it is remarkable in my experience how few cross-cultural negotiations actually become tactical, guerrilla conflicts. In almost all cases, of course, problems do occur along the way—misunderstandings, irritations, confusion—but they are usually resolved before they affect the negotiation for reasons it is important to understand. One reason is that both parties have common goals, interests, and ambitions. Another is that the resources and objectives each side brings to the negotiation are complementary, so mutual interest is always present. A third reason, which I emphasize in this chapter, lies in the effectiveness with which the whole negotiation process and the interpersonal relationships with the other side is managed.

When I look across the spectrum of Japanese–Western

negotiations I am familiar with, a conclusion irresistibly forced on me is that reaching a mutually satisfactory agreement and having it effectively implemented is, more than anything else, a matter of good management skills, common goals, and complementary resources. The cases that follow in this chapter and the next two chapters support this, showing in detail how Japanese–Western negotiations can be effectively brought to a fruitful outcome. They demonstrate that the many Westerners who seek long-term relationships with the Japanese—and avoid opportunistic, tactical behavior as clearly inappropriate—are, most importantly, excellent managers who bring their skills to the special challenges of the cross-cultural negotiating table. We can turn now to look at four cases of effective negotiation with the Japanese to see such managers (Japanese as well as Western) at work.

CASE STUDY: SETTING UP A JOINT VENTURE

Key Points

A well-managed negotiation to set up a complex joint venture of a type not previously attempted in Japan.

Shows problems of cross-cultural communication that arose within the joint U.S.–Japanese project team and how these were resolved.

Shows conceptual and strategic problems that arose and how compromises were worked out that did not seem feasible initially.

Reveals the Japanese government cooperating in many ways with the U.S. side, for example, by changing a law when necessary and devising ways to get around administrative restrictions.

Shows American negotiators being more effective than their Japanese partners in negotiations with Japanese officials.

Mannheim Insurance & Investment Trust of the United States first looked at the Japanese market in 1973, when it was assessing international opportunities for corporate diversification. What it found at the time did not encourage the company to investigate too deeply: the investment climate was not favorable; the only way it could enter the market was through a joint venture with a Japanese partner; the whole investment and insurance industry in Japan was organized in radically different ways from those in the United States and other Western countries; preliminary discussions with Japanese companies yielded no potential compatible partner. Mannheim therefore postponed further study of the Japanese market.

The opportunity to revive the idea of a Japan Mannheim venture resulted from various meetings concerning other matters between Mannheim Chairman Kent J. Fielding, III, and Taro Hattori, chairman of the huge automaker, Mansha Japan K.K. In 1978, Fielding visited Japan and formally requested Mansha to work with Mannheim on a feasibility study of the Japanese market for a joint-venture investment and insurance organization operated in a Western style. Several weeks of discussions followed, and Mansha agreed to work with Mannheim.

The first critical factor was whether or not the Ministry of Finance (MOF) would accept an application for such a business. Hattori himself took on the responsibility for this first approach, receiving a positive answer from MOF within two to three months.

The Feasibility Study: With MOF approval secured, a joint project team was set up, composed of seven to eight members from each side. The project team's main tasks were to answer the following questions:

1. Was there an opportunity for this business in Japan?
The personal investment and insurance market in Japan seemed a mature one, offering few opportunities for an outsider. Penetration, by any standard, was high, with close to 90 percent of households holding some type of long-term investment plan.

2. What personal investment products should be offered?
Until that time, most personal investment in Japan was life insurance of the endowment type. Mannheim, however, was interested in developing the market in Japan for retirement plans. Was there a market for this?

3. Could male sales agents succeed in Japan?
In the United States, investment insurance plans are sold by full-time male agents. In Japan, this is done by female representatives, some 350,000 of them, who mostly work part-time. The task of the project team was to assess the likelihood of success for a full-time team of well-educated, professional, male representatives.

4. What distribution channels would be available in Japan?
One idea was to use Mansha's outlets throughout Japan as the primary sales outlets, but further research soon proved this to be unworkable. Another was to develop male representatives as professional financial consultants (or "investment planners," in line with the practice in Western countries), working from regional offices throughout Japan.

5. How would the new venture be affected by negative reactions in the Japanese business environment, especially those of Japanese investment and life insurance companies?
Mannheim was aware that the Japanese investment industry was raising the usual conservative resistance to a newcomer. How influential would this be and what could be done to counter it? As it turned out, the 1979 request by the U.S. government for liberalization of Japanese financial markets worked very positively in the project's favor.

This market research and feasibility study phase occupied the project team until the second half of 1980, when it submitted its final report and recommendations separately to the two top managements. When the decision to proceed with the formation of the company was made, to begin in January 1981, an entirely new joint team to set up and operate the company was appointed.

The Joint Start-Up Team: Although the initial project team had successfully concluded its work, this was not achieved without some measure of strain, misunderstandings, and conflicting objectives. Many of these problems were to surface again in the start-up team. However, one important point lay in the fact that the senior Mansha men (there were eventually some changes in the project team) were relatively conservative managers who were not enthusiastic about Mannheim's desire to have young and aggressive managers in the new joint venture. The older managers wished to follow conventional Japanese practice, with senior managers in charge, but Mannheim staff were strongly opposed to this. Problems like this threatened the smooth operation of the new management team.

The new team was given two outstanding leaders: Martin O'Brien, fifty-four, vice president of marketing of Mannheim Insurance & Investment Trust, a perceptive businessman who had previous negotiation experience with many foreign governments (but none in Japan) and who held a doctorate in psychology; and Takehiko Kora, thirty-nine, with an American master's degree, one of Mansha's exceptional young managers who had been appointed to a senior management position at the age of thirty-six after assisting the president in Mansha–MITI negotiations and in Japan–U.S. negotiations on exports.

The new team had some immediate problems to overcome. First, they discovered that Japanese law did not permit an exact 50:50 joint venture. They had therefore to approach the Fair Trade Commission to present their arguments in favor of changing the law. This took about four months, after which the law was amended and passed by the Japanese Diet in April 1981.

Second, Mannheim was entering Japan to make a profit. In discussions with MOF, however, the management team discovered that MOF had given administrative guidance to the effect that foreign shareholders could only receive a maximum 10 percent dividend each year. This was insufficient to meet Mannheim's financial goals, and if it was restricted to this level, the enterprise was clearly not worthwhile for Mannheim.

Extensive discussions on this issue took place with the Fair Trade Commission (FTC) and MOF, initially with only the Japanese staff participating, headed by Kora. Negotiations proceeded slowly, partly because Kora was new to dealing with MOF. Although he had long experience in dealing with MITI, he found the bureaucratic style of MOF especially conservative. When O'Brien became dissatisfied with the slow pace, Kora suggested that O'Brien take charge of the negotiations with the two government agencies, with Kora acting as his interpreter and adviser. According to Kora, a remarkable change occurred in the bureacratic attitude as a result of the appearance of a foreign face in the negotiating team.

Such a change is not without precedent and therefore was not entirely unexpected. Japanese officials seem genuinely more comfortable dealing with foreign businessmen, perhaps because foreigners are more relaxed and put the bureaucrats at ease, perhaps because bureaucrats feel greater obligations to help foreign visitors.

With the government negotiating teams now more positive and cooperative, the whole pace quickened. And with Kora there to explain critical points and provide valuable cultural and background information, O'Brien began to obtain a pragmatic and realistic appreciation of the real nature of government attitudes. In particular, he overcame his fear of excessive government involvement in the new venture that might lead to influence and indirect control, no doubt based on vague apprehensions about "Japan, Inc."

By April 1981, a solution proposed by government officials was found to the dilemma. In addition to the 10 percent maximum dividend decreed by MOF administrative guidance,

MOF and FTC would also allow a management assistance fee (determined by an agreed formula) to be paid to the Mannheim head office. With this characteristically creative bureaucratic solution, the first really big hurdle was overcome.

Getting Ready for Business: By June 1981, the new corporation had received its provisional license to do business in Japan, and the management team moved into developing the organization, methods, and staff. From then until the start-up of business, the Japanese–American management team worked together to establish policy and make operational decisions jointly.

Problems continued to plague them, however. For one thing, the official language of the management team was English, and all communications, oral and written, were in English. Although all the Japanese members were adept at reading and writing English, spoken English was difficult for some. This shortcoming had the unfortunate effect of making some of them seem not very intelligent to the Americans, which led to tensions on a day-to-day basis.

Another problem was the habit the young Mansha men had of asking questions of their seniors, as they were accustomed to doing at Mansha. To the Americans, however, this smacked of impudence. One constant irritation for senior Americans was the habit of younger Japanese of saying, regarding a proposal prepared by a senior American, that this or that point was a "problem" (in Japanese, *mondai*). Actually, the nuance of the word "problem" in English is stronger than the Japanese word *mondai*, which means "something that needs looking at further," whereas "problem" means more like "something that is going to be difficult." Moreover, the Japanese custom of replying *"Hai"* ("Yes") or *"Hai wakarimashita"* ("Yes, I understand"), which signified mere comprehension, was interpreted by the Americans to mean that their idea was accepted.

The recruitment of sales agents also involved some problems. The Japanese wanted to employ people with good family and business backgrounds, graduates of well-known universities with previous experience in large corporations. The Americans, on the other hand, were more interested in "braver," more independent men who would take risks and rise on their own merits. In the final hiring process, however, it was found that enough personnel were available who were acceptable to both ways of thinking.

Subsequent Performance: Since beginning business in April 1983, Mansha–Mannheim has enjoyed outstanding success, well beyond its original targets. It has been refreshingly free of disagreements and power struggles, obviously through the difficulties both sides shared during the initial setting up. In spite of introducing a revolutionary marketing approach through the use of professional male sales agents recruited not from school but in mid-career, Mansha–Mannheim has achieved extraordinarily high loyalty levels and a low salesmen turnover that is the envy of Mannheim companies throughout the world. Indeed, Kora, who continues as senior managing director, believes that his company is now "Mannheim's best company worldwide."

Comments

This was a well-managed negotiation headed on both sides by flexible, mature, internationally experienced managers, who are crucial to this type of venture. Without them, it is easy to imagine the cross-cultural misunderstandings—not to mention the regulatory and administrative problems—threatening the whole project. Put another way, a major lesson to learn is that all cross-cultural negotiation is prone to such kinds of difficulties, and that success depends upon how the whole process is handled. Only part of the difficulties stem from cultural sensitivity. Management skill and experience are vitally important, because successful management means effective people management.

CASE STUDY: NEGOTIATING AN OVERSEAS MINING INVESTMENT

Key Points

A well-managed, win-win negotiation.

Shows the importance of friendly personal relationships between the negotiators on each side.

Analyzes Japanese caution and methodicalness, and contrasts these with the North American desire to move more quickly.

Earnings from the trading activities of Toyomitsu, a general trading company, had been declining. In its search for new sources of income, the company became interested in investment in a gold mine in expectation of a future upswing in gold prices. Toyomitsu had investments in various other mining ventures, especially coal and bauxite, but the attraction of precious metals was that they could be immediately sold on the open market, without looking for customers.

In January 1982, the Toyomitsu board approved a search for a gold mine investment. A project team consisting of three engineers led by "Tak" (Takashi) Hasegawa, an experienced minerals business manager, was set up in the Tokyo head office. Its first task was to list up the possible overseas mines for investment, beginning with those in North America. Eventually one candidate, the New Frontier Mining Corporation, was found in Canada, and a subsequent financial analysis showed that New Frontier was 95 percent owned by the Haddock family and that it was clearly undercapitalized and possibly underdeveloped as a mine.

In March 1982, an engineer from Toyomitsu's Chicago office telephoned geologist Lester Haddock, the president and principal shareholder of New Frontier, introduced Toyomitsu, said it was looking for a mine with good investment potential, and asked if he could pay him a visit. Haddock agreed, and two weeks later Tak Hasegawa flew in from Tokyo to accompany the Chicago engineer to Canada.

The meeting opened with Haddock telling the two Japanese that he had had a similar approach, just two weeks previously, from a large American metals conglomerate. But frankly, he said, he hadn't liked the people and felt certain that the conglomerate would want to take over his mine completely, so he had shown them the door.

This frankness pleased the Japanese greatly. They saw Lester Haddock as a big bear of a man, charming, boyish, amusing, but businesslike. They encouraged Haddock to talk about his mine and his ambitions for it, and Tak came to the quick conclusion that his Toyomitsu bosses would be very happy to go into business with this sort of man. When Haddock assured the Japanese that he would on no account let anyone else gain control of New Frontier, Hasegawa could foresee no problem, since Haddock was already prepared, indeed eager, to welcome investment for mine development.

Reassured, Hasegawa made an opening proposal. If, he said, you have some good potential here, we could provide the money needed. The key condition, he said, was that he would need to visit the mine site first to make preliminary geological and mining studies. At the same time, he added, Toyomitsu would like to receive a proposal from Haddock about what he wanted.

For Haddock to display his eagerness for investment so unambiguously, he recounted later, was probably due to two factors. One, he felt comfortable with and was impressed by Tak Hasegawa's approach—calm, clear, to the point, unpretentious, frank, and very different from that of the Americans who had come two weeks before. The other factor was that he had never heard of Toyomitsu until they contacted him, so he had no idea how big they were (in fact, as large as the American mining conglomerate).

From this point on, Haddock became impatient to have the

deal finalized. While the Japanese were still assessing total reserves, Haddock had already made a proposal and was urging a decision. By mid-June, the Japanese had completed their estimate of the total value of mineral in the ground, finding it to be substantial enough to meet their corporate criteria but hardly more than half Haddock's estimate.

Faced with Haddock's higher estimate and his tone of urgency, the Japanese tactically chose to slow down the negotiation. They deferred their formal reply, telling Haddock that they needed more time.

Hasegawa eventually presented Toyomitsu's formal offer in September, having kept Haddock waiting almost three months. He began by explaining Toyomitsu's business practices—its decision-making style, the responsibilities of the negotiation team, and some other special features of Japanese business. (I should point out that it is still extremely rare for a Japanese to do this, a tribute to Hasegawa's excellent command of English and his years of international experience, not to mention his high communication skills.) He then went on to describe Toyomitsu's mining investment activities in Canada, Australia, and Brazil, its investment policy, the fact that this was its first venture into precious metals, and how the New Frontier project rated compared to other projects.

Finally, Hasegawa presented the Toyomitsu proposal. Its key elements were:

1. Toyomitsu asked for 40 percent of New Frontier stock at a price based on its estimate of minable minerals;
2. Exploration and Feasibility Studies: Total cost estimate $5 million;
3. Construction and Development: Assuming the desired reserves and potential were proven, a budget of $45 million;
4. Management Control: Toyomitsu demanded dual control with New Frontier management, with its own people as board members;

5. Profit Distribution: Toyomitsu assumed that it would take three years to get to production, and that the mine would be profitable for ten years (according to estimates at that time). Accordingly, to repay its initial investment, Toyomitsu would require 65 percent in the first four years, and 40 percent (the equity rate) thereafter;

6. Marketing: Toyomitsu would have sole rights to market all minerals mined at New Frontier.

In creating this proposal, Toyomitsu, anticipating a tough negotiation with Haddock, built in a number of opportunities for concessions to be made. For instance, there was the cautious estimate of minable minerals, less than half the figure estimated by Haddock. Likewise, the offer for 40 percent of equity was one it was prepared to increase if necessary.

Three months elapsed from this first face-to-face presentation to final agreement. In this period, Hasegawa and Haddock (by this time on a first-name basis) communicated by telephone every week, while Hasegawa flew from Tokyo each month for lengthy meetings. Most of those meetings were held alone; the two men had quickly come to trust and respect each other and felt that one-on-one meetings would achieve the greatest progress.

In the final agreement, concessions were made on both sides. Haddock eventually accepted a lower provisional estimate of mineral in the ground, came to understand and then accept the rationale of the higher profit distribution for the first four years, and yielded gracefully on the request for marketing rights. In turn, Toyomitsu substantially beefed up its offer price for 40 percent equity and agreed to New Frontier being under the sole control of Haddock.

Comments

Both the Toyomitsu and Mansha–Mannheim cases show professional international managers at work, facilitating detailed agreements with the minimum of friction. In the next case, we also see a similar professional Japanese manager at work behind the scenes to solve a problem that was distressing his company—and we also see the first evidence of how personal connections are used by the Japanese, especially when all else seems to be failing.

CASE STUDY: ACCOMMODATING DIFFERENCES IN POLICY

Key Points

A well-managed negotiation, where the benefits of Japanese indirectness and people-centered strategies pay off.

Contrasts Japanese big-business management style with the more predatory attitude of a Western entrepreneur.

Reveals the management style of a Japanese manager on loan from a top company.

Toyosan K.K. is a medium-size Japanese motor vehicle maker, specializing in light vans and trucks, and it is also part of a larger Toyosan industrial group, which includes a general trading company, electrical appliance company, shipbuilding, mining companies, and so on.

The Toyosan joint venture in the United Kingdom was established in 1974 to import fully assembled vehicles. The principal architects of the joint venture at that time were Neville Butler and the company founder Kotaro Matsudaira, then president, now chairman of Toyosan Japan. Butler (and his colleagues) had a warm and respectful relationship with Matsudaira.

Toyosan U.K. Ltd. is the exclusive distributor of Toyosan vehicles in the United Kingdom, and the Japanese company has a 49 percent interest in it. The British majority share of 51 percent is owned by Butler and his associates.

The financial director of Toyosan U.K. was traditionally a Japanese appointee, and at the time of this case it was Kiyoshi

Suzuki (called Kiyo by the British), who was actually on assignment from Toyosan Trading Company, an affiliate of Toyosan Motors. Suzuki had completed two years of a four-year contract by this time.

Suzuki was the only Japanese among fifty Britons, and in the first year of his stay in the country he devoted himself to becoming fully accepted by his colleagues. With intensive study of idiomatic English, and regular social and sporting contacts, he tried hard to become an Englishman. But all that twelve months of intensive effort brought was exhaustion and a mild nervous breakdown. So Suzuki, giving up the attempt to be accepted as an Englishman, decided to concentrate instead on developing trust and understanding, trying to be totally honest in all aspects of daily business. By the end of his second year in the country, he had succeeded to the point where the English were asking him to mediate their own problems.

Suzuki's success was based partly on his sharp and objective approach to the environment he found himself in. To him, it made sense to think of the British as basically carnivores, who are likely to attack problems quickly and make rapid decisions, in contrast to the more herbivorous Japanese, who tend to ruminate on problems and decisions. In Japan, Suzuki had been a typical company man, concerned not with profits or marketing but with the immediate concerns of his department. Most nights he stayed on to do two hours of overtime.

In the United Kingdom, and especially in the small company he was in, the situation was very different. The Articles of Association of the company said it could do anything. He discovered that the prime concern of the British was not with the business of handling cars but with making profit. This came as a shock to the big-organization man from Tokyo.

There were many other shocks. Suzuki noted that the Japanese were highly gregarious and well-educated compared to the British. Whereas the British had to come from the upper class to make it to the top in business or society, in Japan the son of a *geta* (wooden clog) maker can rise to the top. The British were generally content with their lives and positions while the Japanese were not. Again, the life styles of those at the top in Britain were luxurious and extravagant compared to their counterparts in Japan.

It was at this time, when the Toyosan U.K. business had become so successful, that questions were raised in the House of Commons about the damaging effects of increased Toyosan (and other Japanese) sales upon local industry. Politicians and the media were demanding urgent voluntary ceilings on imports of light vans and trucks.

Inside Toyosan U.K., Butler and his colleagues scoffed at the British government's request for voluntary restraint. Their view was that they would try to sell as many vehicles as they could. The company was their castle, and nobody (not even the government) was going to tell them what to do.

Unable to induce Butler to accept voluntary restraint, Suzuki took the problem to the Toyosan head office in Japan, initially to Goro Abe, director of the international division. After late-night telephone conversations with Abe in Japan, Suzuki would talk with the British directors during the daytime, trying to convince them that Japan *and* Toyosan K.K. would suffer if Toyosan U.K. did not cooperate with its own government. But Butler and company merely replied that they, the Japanese, were cowards when it came to selling cars. Suzuki was especially shocked at this open disrespect for their own government. Moreover, he was disappointed that, unlike previous occasions, this time he was not being listened to, no matter how "nicely and diplomatically" (his words) he spoke to them.

In the end, however, Butler and his fellow directors did agree to impose voluntary quotas. What changed matters was an indirect appeal from the company founder and chairman, Kotaro Matsudaira. Abe had taken the problem to Matsudaira, finding that he (Matsudaira) held the same view as Suzuki and himself. He then arranged for Suzuki to speak directly to Matsudaira, after which a letter was sent from Matsudaira to Butler, putting forth the Japanese viewpoint. When Butler received the letter, he discussed it with Suzuki, asking for more information on the Japanese attitude, and eventually accepted Suzuki's recommendations to impose voluntary quotas.

Comments

Though it was not immediately clear to either Suzuki or Butler, the resolution of this case, and the negotiation dynamic, turned upon the human relationship established between the two key actors—Butler and Matsudaira. Looked at analytically, Matsudaira was the Japanese trump card, to be used only if all else failed.

Although not calculated in this case, it is in fact common for the Japanese to hold back or even conceal their top man for just such final bids for resolution. Unfortunately, perhaps, Western negotiating teams are normally led by the key decision-maker, which leaves no room to use this particular tactic. Of course, when it is the Westerners who are taking the initiative in negotiation, the absence of the key decision-maker on the Japanese side can mean frequent delays as it refers back to head office, delays that often irritate Western businessmen. Toyosan's Suzuki displayed a good degree of tact, diplomacy, and patience in his efforts to persuade the British directors. He was, in my experience, rather typically Japanese in the way he handled the situation. But, admirable as this behavior is, the Japanese do not always behave like this, which is to say that there are in fact a number of "typical" Japanese behavior styles. Which one is used depends in good part on the stage reached in the negotiation.

CASE STUDY: NIPPON TEXACOM

Key Points

Although this case had a satisfactory outcome for both sides, the American manager involved was never sure until near the end that anything he did would be effective.

Shows how easy it is for Westerners new to Japan to become culturally disoriented, which inhibits their ability to analyze and assess problematic business situations.

It is easy to offend—unintentionally—some Japanese.

As in the Mansha–Mannheim case, the American manager, once he began to understand the cultural nature of business problems in Japan, was more effective than his Japanese staff in dealing with Japanese government officials.

The number of viable negotiation options you can think up in a Japanese negotiation situation depends upon the richness and realism of your understanding of corporate life, culture, and human psychology.

Much of the success of the Toyomitsu and Toyosan cases stem from the good personal relationships between the two sides, without which agreement would not have been achieved so easily. In the next case, however, good human relations were only of minor importance. Even though relationships between the two sides were always businesslike, and despite there being little that was culturally based, in fact no personal friendships developed.

This case stemmed from the concern of Nippon Texacom Inc., the subsidiary of a large foreign company in Japan, over the security of its internal telephone conversations and facsimiles. Unlike other advanced countries, the telephone system in Japan (at the time of this dispute) did not provide what is called DID, or Direct Inward Dialling. DID permits a subscriber with one trunk line to attach up to, say, ten to fifteen extensions to it. Systems providing DID that are familiar to

Westerners are the PBX and CBX, which permit all internal calls, as well as incoming and outgoing calls, to be routed through them. Japan provided the CENTREX system, where the switching between internal calls—for example, from one desk extension to the next—is done through the telephone company and the lines it owns. Not only was this good business for the Japanese telephone companies (since, unlike the DID or PBX system, you paid for every internal call under the CENTREX system), it also meant that many internal calls could actually be routed through lines in other buildings, some of which were owned by Nippon Texacom's Japanese competitors and rented from them by the Japanese telephone system.

The point of the story is that Nippon Texacom began to obtain disquieting evidence that its lines were being tapped because information carried in the Japanese-language media could only have come from an internal "mole" or a tap. A "mole" was soon ruled out when a test was conducted, which then confirmed the "tap" theory.

The only effective strategy to prevent taps was to discard the CENTREX system and install a PBX system that would give complete security to internal calls. Accordingly, a senior Nippon Texacom telecommunication specialist, Terry Saviola, took charge of this project, one of his major tasks being to negotiate the divestment of the existing CENTREX system, as well as the termination of long-term ten-year rental contracts for the associated handsets and relay boxes. Saviola first approached the handset and box renters, and those negotiations proceeded smoothly, within the cost parameters already established in Texacom.

In the meantime, Saviola had his staff review the contract position with the Japanese telephone system, and was pleased to be told that the only relevant clause in the very simple contract was one that allowed for cancellation in thirty days. Seeing this as a simple matter, he instructed his Japanese subordinates to inform the Japanese telephone authorities that

Nippon Texacom would be soon activating the thirty-day cancellation clause.

His Japanese subordinates returned from that meeting with glum faces. The telephone authorities, they said, insisted that they had an *implicit* ten-year contract with Nippon Texacom. In fact, they argued, it was because Texacom had entered into a ten-year agreement that they had especially invested heavily in expanded services. The Japanese Texacom employees, as dutiful citizens, informed Saviola that there was nothing that Texacom could now do but accept the government position and continue with the CENTREX system.

Saviola was, shall we say, displeased with the conclusions, not to mention the report of his subordinates. Having been in Japan less than twelve months, however, he felt helpless and extremely disoriented. The senior expatriate manager to whom he reported took a cold and unfriendly attitude to the whole matter. Saviola tried to probe his Japanese colleagues to search for alternative ideas, but they proved too wedded to the idea of obeying the government view.

Eventually, Saviola was introduced to a foreign negotiation consultant in Tokyo, with whom he discussed the situation at length. As a result, Saviola developed the confidence to negotiate directly and alone with the Japanese, using only a professional interpreter.

A few days later he met with the same group within the telephone organization as had his subordinates. The negotiations started on a friendly but firm note, with both parties holding out for their previous positions. But as soon as Saviola mentioned Texacom's security concern (in anticipation of sympathy), the mood changed. The senior Japanese turned red with anger.

"Are you accusing we Japanese of listening in to your conversations? Do you dare imply that we Japanese are thieves? What about your own people? It is a disgrace for you people, the invited guests in our country, to slander us in this way."

Saviola saw that he had touched a very sensitive nerve of national pride. There was nothing more to do that day. He apologized sincerely and left.

But just when it appeared that all was lost, Lady Luck, as it were, arrived on the scene. First, as a result of government-level Japan–Western telecommunications negotiations, the Japanese government finally decided to privatize the telecommunications industry. Second, after further analysis and review of his own negotiations, Saviola identified a telephone system executive of a much higher rank than the angry bureaucrat and was able to arrange an interview with him. From the combination of these two factors came an entirely new and flexible response to Texacom's concerns. The insistence on an implicit long-term contract was abandoned and the thirty-day cancellation clause was honored.

For the most part, this negotiation was clearcut and businesslike. Two points are probably cultural. The sensitivity on a point of national honor and rectitude is one. (In fact, Texacom had never suspected the telephone system of the tapping, only its competitors.) The other may be the Japanese insistence that there really was a ten-year contract. I say "may be" because this seems to me to have been merely tactical on the part of the Japanese, similar in kind to assertions by other Japanese in other situations, such as the sugar dispute with Australia (Chapter 4).

Comments

These cases support the unsurprising conclusion that cultural sensitivity may play only a modest role in the outcome of Japanese–Western negotiations. However, the factors that were more significant were also diverse, ranging from well-planned offers that anticipate future needs for concessions (as in the Toyomitsu case) down to the use of appeals to higher authorities (with Texacom). Most important of all, these cases were dealt with by true professionals, cooperative, systematic, emotionally mature, strategic, and resolute in their drive to solve problems as they arise. In doing this, they not only sustain their motivation to treat the negotiations as game-type—safeguarding against any escalation into purely tactical behavior—but they also present an effective model for the execution of international negotiation.

Chapter 3

The Japanese Negotiating with Foreign Friends

Friendly relationships are deliberately sought after by the Japanese, and they often stress how much they desire a long-term relationship with others. Ordinarily, when they deal on a basis of equality with a foreign organization, there will be an underlying brisk, businesslike approach by the Japanese. They will expect both parties to be treated with meticulous fairness, with demands and needs from both sides being acknowledged and, as far as possible, met.

The two cases presented in this chapter reflect, in my experience, broader tendencies in the way Japanese organizations relate to friends or intimates, tendencies not often observed in the behavior of Western organizations. One tendency is the desire to stress fairness to the other side more than they usually would—on such grounds as "we are a nonprofit organization, so we should not think of profit or advantage over our friends," or "we are all part of the same family, so it is not too important to bargain hard to get a better deal." Although they bring such attitudes to the negotiating table, it is often a shock to find that the foreign side does not share the same feeling but behaves like a typical independent organization. The failure to meet their expectations creates negative emotions that take time to be resolved by the Japanese, just as it takes time, and perhaps a special sensitivity, for Westerners to realize that the Japanese they are facing may be ready to be more accommodating to them than to complete outsiders. The emergence of problems like these can move such negotiations into a kind of cross-cultural limbo where neither side is sure how best to negotiate with the other. In the midst of this uncertainty, the belief can arise that one's own negotiating style is inferior to that of the other side, and therefore that one should borrow the other side's style. How this works out, we shall soon see.

In a broader perspective, however, negotiations with friendly or related organizations are resolved amicably and effectively, even though—as in the Mansha–Mannheim case and others—problems of misunderstanding, resentment, and confusion can arise along the way.

CASE STUDY: TWO BROADCASTING ORGANIZATIONS

Key Points

The Japanese are most flexible and ready to compromise when they deal with organizations they regard as part of the family.

When negotiators lose confidence about how to handle demands, they may retreat to imitating the other side's offensive or defensive style.

In family-type negotiations, the Japanese may tolerate without overt complaint behavior that would otherwise offend them.

This negotiation took place between two major broadcasting organizations, one in Japan (called JBC) and one from overseas (called FBS). FBS is an extremely large company, but JBC matches it in size, so both companies wield immense power in the broadcasting industry. JBC has more ties with this particular foreign company than with any other, mainly through past successful negotiations and common interests in some nonprofit subcompanies within FBS. Consequently, there are friendly personal ties between the two companies at the corporate level.

FBS approached JBC to cooperate on the production of a program commemorating a major war anniversary. The program, to be jointly broadcast by JBC and FBS, would undoubtedly gain worldwide attention and was of great importance to FBS.

The two broadcasting companies had worked together exchanging information for many years before this negotiation. However, because one company exists for profit, and one company is legally considered a nonprofit organization, a specially created branch of JBC is used for all such negotiations.

In January, FBS made the actual proposal to JBC, and for the next three months, preliminary ideas were discussed by telephone and telex. In March, FBS staff were sent to Tokyo to discuss the proposed program. Discussions were in English without the help of interpreters. In June, FBS asked JBC to join in the research for the program, and although JBC did not say yes explicitly, it went ahead and did the research. JBC also provided cost estimates of services it would provide to produce and transmit the special. In July, a major plane crash caused a diversion of FBS funds from research into news coverage, and FBS asked JBC to lower the production cost of the program.

Because the negotiations were dealing with a cooperative effort rather than an actual trade of goods or services, the situation was not particularly competitive (at least from the Japanese viewpoint). The two companies had often dealt with each other in negotiation situations, so the JBC people had (they said) preconceived notions about what the Americans would be like. JBC also made it clear that its own people had a clear negotiation style that was "very Japanese," while the FBS people lived up to the Western "direct and to the point" style of negotiating. Given these differences, and notwithstanding the goodwill of both parties toward each other, problems arose, among them the following.

FBS people had a tendency to ask JBC to make various bookings, including those for hotels, and then cancel them at the last minute. They also frequently changed schedules, causing enormous difficulties for JBC. Believing they were essentially sister organizations, JBC accepted these changes without demur, and even when this meant cash loss to JBC, it paid out of its own pocket without informing FBS.

Another problem was the routine scheduling difficulties caused by the extra work. FBS wanted a live broadcast. However, because JBC only had limited studios and equipment available, it was hard to work out production hours. FBS wanted to work between 2 P.M. and 4 A.M., because these hours suited the foreign broadcasts. While this was very difficult for JBC, such was the pressure exerted by FBS that JBC eventually accommodated the foreigners. There was also trouble within the FBS administration. FBS had an office in Tokyo that dealt with JBC, but requests also came from the overseas head office, and sometimes the various requests conflicted.

The negotiation of technical arrangements between the two countries posed some difficulty. JBC had access to only a few satellites, and FBS wanted the use of one, so JBC had to refuse other broadcasters. FBS had to reserve the satellites far in advance, intending to use them for about two hours a day for pre-coverage and for the entire day on the actual anniversary. However, FBS's constant change of plans led to cancellation of the satellite time on very short notice. FBS would overbook satellite time and then feel free to cancel, causing tremendous trouble to JBC and its affiliates. This, said JBC people, was the biggest problem during the entire process.

Comments

The JBC lead negotiator expected his team to negotiate in a typical Japanese way that emphasizes intuitive understanding of the other side and the analysis of nonverbal behavior. He felt that in negotiation both the Westerners and the Japanese revealed a great deal about how they felt without using words.

This led to the Japanese being quieter and more receptive throughout the negotiations.

Because the negotiations were held entirely in English, the Japanese had problems about how to refuse FBS requests. Before the long, difficult negotiation began, JBC people were totally unable to say no because they felt that it was very impolite. By the end of the negotiation, they had learned, with some repugnance, how to say no. At one point late in the talks, the Japanese began to say no to everything proposed by FBS. This change confounded the Westerners, who were unprepared for it.

For a time, the Japanese decided to use the American negotiation style in important meetings, but in most cases they found themselves incapable of carrying this out in practice. Even those individual Japanese negotiators who forced themselves to act like this felt very unhappy about their performance afterwards.

In reflecting on the negotiations, JBC felt as though it had had to yield to about 80 percent of FBS's demands. A major factor in this was the fact that JBC was a nonprofit, service organization. Even though JBC yielded often, it rationalized this by saying that the process was helping in the exchange and development of more programs, and by this means JBC was providing a better service to the Japanese public.

CASE STUDY: NEGOTIATING WITH YOUR KID BROTHER

Key Points

In-family negotiations involve a high level of commitment on both sides to achieving agreement.

Westerners working for Japanese companies tend to imitate the Japanese, probably as a normal result of adapting to the culture.

As in the previous case, the Japanese will tolerate behavior from "friends" that would be viewed as offensive from out-siders.

*Mutual imitation occurred as a result of loss of confidence.

This second "between friends" negotiation occurred between Hitoba Corporation, the parent company, and its U.S.-based subsidiary, Hitoba Systems of America. The two companies had never negotiated before, and in preparation they held several meetings to work out preliminaries. The actual negotiation, which involved millions of dollars and lasted nearly a year, concerned a proposal by the subsidiary to buy cash dispensers for use in banks throughout the United States. Hitoba was to manufacture and ship these cash dispensers while the subsidiary would market, distribute, and sell them to banks.

Hitoba gathered much of its information in the preliminary meetings, a procedure it often employed to decide which projects had a better chance of profitability, especially where sums of millions of dollars were concerned.

In addition to this, Hitoba always made it a practice to study the market in which its negotiation partner was selling, in this case actually helping to research the American market for cash dispensers. Its aim was to be fully informed before commencing negotiation.

The opening stage of the negotiations was held in Japan at Hitoba's headquarters. The American subsidiary began with requests for products with very detailed specifications, covering elements of styling, mechanics, and functions that had to be met. Initially, price was not an item of the negotiation, as Hitoba had to approve and consider the specification proposals before negotiating the price. After these opening discussions, Hitoba held internal meetings to discuss production, costs, and other aspects. Through these Hitoba found that it would encounter many problems with materials and specifications that would affect subsequent price negotiations. Despite these problems, Hitoba decided to accept the American requests and approved further negotiations.

Each team of negotiators consisted of six to ten members. The initial stages were relatively smooth, though some conflict arose out of the very specific demands and requirements of the subsidiary. The mood at this stage was relaxed and easy on the surface, but many felt undercurrents of tension. The biggest difficulty encountered here was the frequent recesses taken by the main company to discuss the subsidiary's proposals.

On the Japanese side there was only one leader/spokesman, whereas the Americans had more fluidity and less focus, with each member contributing opinions and ideas. Moreover, the American team seemed to have more authority than the head office team in making decisions. The Japanese side complained of having to negotiate not only with the Americans but also with their superiors. The lesser authority of the Japanese side was a source of many conflicts and tensions experienced in this opening stage. The American team, which had only this project to worry about, could devote all its time and effort to it, whereas the Japanese team members had other responsibilities and were not always able to work as much on the project as they would have wished.

After the preliminaries concerning design, production, and styling were worked out, the negotiations proceeded to dealing with specific details. The second round of negotiations took place in a new locale, in Fremont, California, where the subsidiary was based. This seemed to brighten the mood of the negotiations, with the Japanese team looking more relaxed and the talks proceeding smoothly, though conflicts over price became a main issue. (This change of locale, it turned out later, had been a strategic one on the part of the Hitoba parent company to try to ease tensions.)

With design problems all but settled, a price for the dispensers was next on the negotiating agenda. As noted earlier, Hitoba knew it would run into some problems with material availability and production costs, and it used these arguments to begin initial negotiations over price. While the Japanese side was arguing that it would have to have a higher price to meet costs, the American side argued that the market called for a much lower price since competition was stiff. This haggling continued for several days and caused some delays, but despite this the negotiations were never seriously threatened and no major conflicts arose. By this time, the Japanese had also become more accustomed to the earnest, direct, and aggressive styles of the Western negotiators, and anticipated this behavior from the new team in the United States. However, what surprised the Japanese was that, when faced with a conflict, the Americans seemed to switch to a classic Japanese style of avoidance and indirectness. These tactics suggested that the Americans were preparing more seriously for their negotiations with the Japanese by trying to adapt their style to a Japanese one.

In the final stages of the negotiation, both sides resolved the outstanding price and design problems to their mutual satisfaction, and the negotiations ended with both sides making concessions, but each satisfied with the outcome.

Comments

These last two cases demonstrate a dilemma that seems to me to be growing with the increase in cross-cultural negotiations. What is the appropriate way to negotiate with foreign friends? In both cases, the Japanese felt a strong sense of obligation to be fair and to be more effective communicators in the Western sense. In the first case, they tried bravely to be direct, but secretly hated it. In the second case, the Americans, being untypically indirect, were also hoping to communicate in a more effective, less contentious way. But they also felt they were behaving unnaturally.

The behavior in these cases reflects a broad and increasing trend over the last twenty years or so. The Japanese have found the Western "hot" style of forceful argumentation, deductive logic, and tactical bargaining to be intimidating, just as Westerners have been perplexed by the Japanese "cool" style of non-negotiable demands, indifference to time, and ambiguity of response.

As a result, what I have seen happening in both Japan and the West, is that each side imitates the other in the hopes of achieving more leverage, with the Japanese often adopting a combative, argumentative style, and the Westerners a defensive, non-negotiable, indifference-to-time style. Each side feels tied to a basically friendly, mutually obligatory, but persistently frustrating relationship. In the search for a more effective way of negotiating, both sides can go to extremes in outdoing the other with their borrowed styles, so that they end up irritating and perplexing each other even more.

In other words, this style of borrowing turns out to be a tactic, a gimmick, a mere formula for negotiators who are still not sure how to adopt a true problem-solving approach to difficult international situations in trade or diplomacy.

What are the key elements in such a problem-solving approach? Amicable communication between friends is a good start, but after that experienced managers, effective ideas, and human know-how to solve negotiation problems are needed. Gimmicks such as imitating what the other side is doing, especially if this is irritating and affects our composure, have to be guarded against. One problem with gimmicks is that they often exacerbate the conflict. Another problem is that they tend to be overdone: the indirect, avoidance tactic becoming some kind of "master tactic," and the "arguing every last point syndrome" becoming a magical technique for outdoing the foreigner.

Chapter 4

Managing Japanese Accounts

It is common to think of negotiation as a simple buy–sell activity that is focused on achieving a specific objective and is concluded when a contract is signed. In fact, many negotiation activities are better thought of as permanent or ongoing processes. The term used to describe people who represent a company in its dealings with a client on a full-time basis is "account managers," and the client they work with is the "account." This chapter will concentrate on the special problems experienced by Western account managers in dealing with their Japanese clients, with examples of both success and failure. First, let us look at two cases of successful account managers in Japan.

CASE STUDY: THE IMPORTANCE OF KNOWING JAPAN

Key Points

Establishing your own representative office in Tokyo is important.

Managers who understand Japan and speak Japanese can operate hands-on in Japan.

High-level skills in human relations are critical in dealing with the Japanese.

The Neuerbach Forestry Products Company of Canada

established a Tokyo subsidiary in 1963. Its initial interest lay in exporting logs and woodchips to Japan, but since the late 1970s half of their Japan sales has been in finished products, including liner board and newsprint.

The chief executive officer (CEO) of Neuerbach Japan has always been a Canadian fluent in Japanese. The present CEO, Humphrey Dewey, originally came to Japan as a young missionary, and today is responsible for the Northeast Asia region. In Japan, Dewey is involved in almost daily negotiations that are conducted in Japanese without interpretation. These may concern woodchip contracts that run for five to seven years, different ways of pricing liner boards, or price revisions arising from the strengthening of the yen.

Dewey's job is almost entirely account management, dealing regularly with long-established customers. Nonetheless, in preparing for each major negotiation, the situations of even the oldest accounts are carefully reviewed and a strategy team is formed.

Depending on the length of the contract under negotiation, his team will first try to gauge where the market is going, based on information gathered. Second, the internal goals of Neuerbach are reviewed, such as its current position in the market and whether it wants to increase that market share. If there is a desire to do so, the team might try to obtain more of that increase from one company than from another. This could determine how strongly Neuerbach will be willing to bargain in the negotiation. The status of the firm with which it is negotiating is also investigated, that is, its financial position, market share, current management structure, long-term goals, and so on. Another factor taken into consideration prior to negotiation is the general compatibility of the company, especially if Neuerbach is looking for long-term ties.

When dealing with Japanese corporations, Dewey generally takes the written word less seriously than his personal ties with the company. Once personal trust is established, cooperation increases and more can be accomplished in the negotiations. The primary purpose of the written word is to satisfy the legalities involved.

According to Dewey, it can sometimes be difficult to identify the real leader of the Japanese team. It is important to be able to do this because even though the Japanese make a lot of decisions on a group basis, the nominal leader might be somewhat of a "maverick" and therefore delay progress. Another factor to take into consideration is that leadership can swing from one member to another depending on the issue at hand, be it finance or shipping or whatever, a situation that occurs more with Japanese teams than Western ones. At times the leader might say very little and at other times he might do most of the talking.

Dewey stresses that rather than just selling the product, product servicing plays a much bigger role in the success of a company in Japan than it does in the West. He packages a variety of services, including letting his Japanese clients know what is going on technologically and frequently involving their people in quality control, and so on.

It is important, adds Dewey, within one's own organization "to have a common train of thought and a common goal." If the Japanese sense any disagreement in your ranks, it will discourage them, and could lead to a failed negotiation. The Japanese are very good at detecting such disagreement, so it is important to be aware of unity within your group. As the Japanese are more tolerant of ambiguity than Americans, it is essential that no matter which language is used, the ideas from either side are clearly understood. This is particularly important with new clients.

Sometimes a meeting will end without any clear indication as to whether or not it was a success, a situation much easier for Japanese to tolerate than Westerners. However, once a certain amount of trust is established between the two parties, things tend to go very smoothly, and positive or negative feelings are more easily detectable. Often it is necessary for points to be conveyed in both English and Japanese to minimize misunderstandings. Neuerbach has clients who speak good English and those who speak none at all, so it likes to have both Japanese and Westerners in its negotiating teams.

Dewey feels that the Japanese, more accustomed to negotiation than North Americans, are also much better at it. Within Canadian society, the number of occasions requiring negotiation are very few, perhaps limited to the parent–teenager or labor–management relationship. "Other than that we are somewhat naive in negotiation," he concludes. Prices in North America are, for the most part, fixed, and any fluctuation tends to make Americans and Canadians a little suspicious. In Japan, on the other hand, intimate, face-to-face. and detailed negotiation is a part of everyday life.

Comments
As others have pointed out, the Japanese are no more or less capable at negotiation than anyone else. They are often constrained by being factional in character, not unified. Dewey, as mentioned earlier, strongly urged that negotiation teams should be unified, but it is not only Westerners who need to learn this.

An example of the lack of unity among the Japanese is found in the negotiations for the purchase of iron ore for Japanese steel mills, which has traditionally been handled by Nippon Steel on behalf of thirteen domestic steel makers. Although in appearance the steel makers offer a united front, some of the big foreign iron ore producers with liaison offices in Japan have discovered that this is only a veneer, and that the Japanese have frequently been confused over demands and strategies. Producers with liaison offices in Tokyo have been generally able to deal more successfully with Nippon Steel than those who do not have offices.

Dewey demonstrates the benefits of residing on the spot and

being fluent in the language. One of the other big weaknesses of foreigners resident overseas has been their lack of a comprehensive recognition of what the account manager's job entails. Many have a background in technology or engineering, rather than management, and lack those skills in human relations that are so important in Japan. The successful account manager for Japan must also keep closely in touch with changes in the world's most fiercely competitive and fastest-changing market, so that he is able to fine-tune his client services effectively. The next case presents a picture of just such a successful account manager in Japan.

CASE STUDY: A PROFESSIONAL AMERICAN NEGOTIATOR

Key Points

Being well prepared, knowing what to do at each stage of negotiation, and managing the smooth flow of the negotiation are the keys to success.

Observing and understanding Japanese nonverbal behavior gives non-Japanese a real edge.

Being on the spot is essential to successful long-term negotiation with the Japanese.

Calco, an American metals company has close to one hundred production facilities in twenty countries, and its product may be shipped to Japan from one of many countries throughout the world. Calco's general manager in charge of sales for the whole of the Asian region is Robert Midway, who began working for the company as a salesman in the American Midwest, then served in the world headquarters in Los Angeles before his present appointment to Japan in 1979. Midway has been outstandingly successful in his Tokyo position. An accomplished salesman and negotiator, a polished communicator, and a highly perceptive judge of people, his views on negotiating with the Japanese and his negotiating method contain many valuable hints for businessmen who wish to become more effective international negotiators.

Midway directs a staff of Japanese account managers and is also personally involved in all metal contract negotiations with Japanese buyers, as well as advising other members of his corporation's worldwide affiliates on how to deal with the Japanese. The company maintains continuous telex and telephone communication with its world headquarters and such key centers as London, Pittsburgh, Rio, and Melbourne, and it receives daily reports from these and other centers on market fluctuations, supply, and inventory, as well as background news on markets, competitors, and clients. Calco's intelligence function is on a par with that of any major Japanese general trading company.

Although Calco negotiates a number of different contracts for metals, the type to be described here is what is called an informal frame contract. This is relatively long-term, where Calco agrees to deliver so many tons per month, with the price negotiated on a quarterly or, less frequently, monthly basis.

In preparing for any negotiation, Calco consults numerous data concerning world prices of the product. The most important of these are the London Commodities Market quotations, which at the present time serve as a basis for negotiation everywhere in the world. Moreover, prices are periodically published in the Japanese press, and other data are quoted prices from metals traders and informally reported "street" prices.

In addition to price information, inventory data are also important for the simple reason that an increase in inventory will reinforce the bargaining power of the buyer, while a decrease in inventory will increase the bargaining power of the seller. Inventory data that are regarded as important are world inventory, Japanese domestic inventory, and a customer's own inventory. Inventory data are also used by both sides for predictions of future market trends.

Midway uses these data to decide the price range he will negotiate within, especially his opening, or "offer," price, and his minimum price. He develops his arguments and the picture of the market and its trends to justify his price offer. He also tries, he says, "to put myself in the [Japanese] customer's shoes and understand how he is likely to view things." By doing this, he can more fully predict what they will ask for and prepare for that. It is this step that Midway feels is the most important in preparing for negotiations.

It is worthwhile to point out here that buyers will almost certainly have the same market, supply, and inventory data available as Midway. Negotiating skill shows up in the way the data are used to develop a position and support it.

Calco usually has a team of two people, Midway and one of his Japanese account managers. On the client side, the team will comprise four to six people. If the Japanese team is from a trading company, in two out of three cases the most senior Japanese will be a division manager (*buchō*) and the lowest level will be a section manager (*kachō*). In other cases, the highest-ranking person will be a director (*torishimariyaku*), who will probably also be a divisional general manager (*honbuchō*). If the client is a metal end-user, a director is always present. It is interesting to look at the composition of the teams and to what extent they include someone who is able to make decisions on the spot. In Calco's case, Midway has complete authority to make decisions. In the Japanese case, when a director is not present, any decision will have to be referred to someone higher.

Meetings, conducted either in English or English with Japanese interpretation, may last for a minimum of two hours, a whole day, or, on occasions, can go on for weeks. However, in general, the longer the relationship between Calco and its Japanese client, the shorter the meetings.

Negotiations invariably start with each side giving an opening presentation ranging from fifteen to forty-five minutes.

When Calco speaks first, it talks about the strength of the market, both now and in the future, envisions demand for the product remaining strong but production not quite catching up. Then the talk continues on the advantages of dealing with Calco, an international giant, for if there is a problem with one source, it can divert the order to another source to be filled efficiently. Throughout his opening statement, Midway always strives to convey a positive, pleasant impression, an important approach because Japanese clients know how to paint a very different picture of the market, one of falling prices, rising inventories, overproduction, with the prospect of prices going down further.

After the opening statements have been made, one side will mention a price, followed by a counteroffer from the other side. The Japanese customers refer to theirs as a "target price," while Calco calls it an "offer price." Usually, they are about $70 apart, with the customer's being the lower. Midway says—surprisingly, in view of comments usually made to the contrary—that he has to start with a higher price than he expects to get more often in Japan than in other countries because his Japanese customers always try to bargain. This drive to bargain seems unusual in Japan, especially among customers in the Kantō (Tokyo–Yokohama) region, but is much commoner in the Kinki (Nagoya) and Kansai (Osaka) regions. Midway believes that metal buyers have taught themselves to bargain, after contacts with Westerners and with Chinese from Malayasia and Singapore, and that bargaining was not, originally, part of the Kantō area business culture.

The next step is what Midway calls "the discussion and the rhetoric." After bargaining, both sides come to an agreement on price and other contract details. Price is the last item to be settled, after delivery conditions and rates, port of shipment, payment terms, and product specifications are concluded. Midway maintains a policy of being flexible in these areas, so that he can remain firmer on price.

In this stage of the negotiation, Midway sees the importance of the sincerity of the arguments used. The more involved and concerned the negotiators appear, the more smoothly the negotiations progress.

Midway's perceptiveness about his Japanese clients stems from his sensitivity to Japanese "body language" and its meaning in this critical stage of the negotiation. Much, he says, can be learned from posture, tilting and nodding of the head, facial expression, and especially the eyes, which offer valuable clues as to how the negotiations are progressing. He watches the conversations among team members, noting that signs such as "inhaling of air" or "sucking air through the teeth" usually indicate a soft spot in the Japanese negotiating position.

There are times when it is important to break off negotiations either for a temporary recess to review progress (which is usually done by the Japanese) or because it seems no one is getting anywhere, and a break is needed by both sides to rethink positions and strategies. Knowing just when to break is something one learns to sense, says Midway. The signs can come out of body language or from the state of the dialogue. Westerners need to learn the positive benefits to be gained from such recesses.

Some Japanese customers from time to time attempt to obtain additional price concessions by the use of what Midway describes as "illogical" claims. For instance, the customer might take a price from a worst-case situation, and say, "There was this case yesterday where the product sold for only such and such yen" (that is, well below the price that Midway was proposing on the day). Usually this would be a case of "distressed merchandise," that is, a shipment where there was something wrong with the documents, or the weights, or the analysis. It is only by being constantly in touch with the marketplace, and knowing about such cases, that a negotiator is able to handle such objections promptly, calmly, and authoritatively.

As the bargaining brings the two parties close together, the

Japanese side may suddenly say, "Well, you know we are a long-term customer, so we want a long-term discount." To handle this, Midway studiously avoids becoming involved in discussing the issue at all, but returns to his main argument about how his side had arrived at the price in the first place. Another example of a tactic used in these later stages is, "Buying at the market price is unacceptable to us." An answer such as "My company is committed to the market process as the only way to ensure fair trading" may be good enough to handle this type of demand.

Asked whether he thinks that this type of behavior is "typically Japanese," Midway calculated that it was only one or two customers who did this all the time, with perhaps two or three others doing it occasionally, out of fifteen or so major clients he deals with regularly. Therefore, he does not consider it typically Japanese.

Midway says that knowing when it is time to conclude the negotiation is something one learns to sense or feel. At this point, his philosophy dictates that you make your last concession and agree on a price. Until that point, he has given strong arguments, but now, as seller, it is time to weaken a little. What he aims for is an agreement where the customer feels he has ended up "winning," a feeling that comes from a final concession by the seller. There is, he says, also an element of "face-saving" here, leading to better post-negotiation feelings and enhanced future prospects.

Midway observes that the oft-noted distinction that the Japanese are more concerned about the relationship, Westerners more about the written contract, is only generally true in his experience. He says that in dealing with Japanese customers, he tries to incorporate differences of viewpoint, but there are often exceptions. Increasingly, he finds that Japanese customers are feeling the need for some type of contract, although it is a much more general instrument than in the West. "Letters of understanding" are also common, although he had one recent case where the new (Japanese) general manager said that he wanted a real contract in the future. It is also generally true in his experience that it is not the document but the relationship that is important with the Japanese, and the longer the relationship, the more secure the business.

AN ACCOUNT MANAGER IN TROUBLE

Not every foreign account manager has been as successful as Midway. Gordon Hathaway, an Englishman who previously served in Chicago and London, has been an account manager in the Tokyo office of an international commodities house for the past eighteen months and observes many differences between a commodities account manager's job in the West and in Japan. In his words:

> It takes a long time for the Japanese to get to know you....They are not really comfortable with me or any other foreigner face to face. They are always on guard, and it is not sufficient just to have the goods and the right price. In the West, clients look mainly to short-term profits, but here the emphasis is on personal relations, and for a very specific reason: the Japanese expect to get something back in the long run. In fact, being close to Japanese clients in itself influences your readiness to compromise and concede.

Hathaway says he has found that the Japanese he deals with use the enhanced personal relationship to get "under his guard," to demand concessions that could easily be rejected on purely rational grounds, but not so easily on emotional grounds, which can be appealed to in long-term relationships. Although he is constantly seeking ways to avoid yielding to Japanese nonrational appeals, he ruefully admits that he is barely holding his own.

"Dealing with Japanese buyers," says Hathaway, "is like mental fencing. And they are better at it than most." Even though he deals regularly with the same people, Hathaway concedes that he has only achieved a superficial friendliness.

"I can't read their faces at all," he says with exasperation. "They discuss points in Japanese in front of me, and I don't understand. Most of all, I've learned to beware of 'come-ons' from the Japanese. Never accept their promises, for even gentlemen's agreements hold only for a limited time. If they are annoyed with you for any reason, they suddenly become unavailable. On the other hand, they will never hesitate to complain."

Hathaway said that one of his biggest shocks was the refusal of the Japanese to accept a proposal for a new method of calculating foreign exchange rates that would have saved them $40,000 per year. Hathaway explained it once, slowly and carefully, for one and a half hours. His clients then discussed it in private, and, after a considerable time, returned and asked him to repeat his explanation. They listened carefully and again asked many questions, but in the end they still would not agree to his recommendation. Two weeks later, he was told that their final decision was not to accept it, leaving him mystified, irritated, and a little contemptuous.

Were Hathaway's reactions justified? According to Anthony E. Zaroom, an American lawyer and Japan specialist, the key factor in such a case is not Japanese conservatism or caution, but the difficulty of obtaining the required consensus within a Japanese organization in order to put new ideas into practice. For instance, he once advised a Japanese company about a joint real estate investment in the United States. In order to save the Japanese company $5 million to $6 million in taxes, he recommended that it form a partnership rather than a corporation. The Japanese executive who received Zaroom's recommendation, however, showed no sign of pleasure at this. Instead, he complained that as the original consensus within his company had been to set up a corporation, he would have endless difficulties trying to change that. Finally, the Japanese executive recommended the formation of a corporation against Zaroom's advice.

Hathaway's problem may have stemmed from a similar dilemma. However financially attractive a new recommendation might be, the biggest concern of the people who receive it may be the objections they foresee in their own companies about any changes. Decision-making based on consensus often becomes a positive hindrance to efficient management.

Zaroom points out that representatives of Japanese companies who receive advice from consultants may be members of the decision-making group but, for various reasons, may not have the opportunity to communicate the advice precisely and in detail to key decision-makers. Thus, the final decision may be taken by senior managers who are essentially uninformed or unskilled in the specialist area. Most foreign consultants can cite cases like this, as can Japanese consultants.

One complaint against the Japanese that is commonly voiced by foreign businessmen is that the Japanese do not hesitate to ask for price reductions and other concessions when they are in trouble, but tend to be deaf to similar requests from foreigners. A recent article in the *American Chamber of Commerce in Japan Journal* cites the case of a Japanese firm that contracted to buy coal from British Columbia. On the basis of the twenty-five-year contract and an agreed price, the Canadians built roads and a port. Then the Japanese reduced their price, making the project no longer viable for the Canadians.

Some years ago, Australian woodchip exporters to Japan maintained supplies at the contracted price when world prices skyrocketed. A few years later, when world prices dropped to a very low level, the Japanese immediately requested a significant reduction in the contract price.

Indeed, it has long been accepted in Australia that Japanese steel mills deliberately encouraged overinvestment in the iron ore industry so that the world market would be in a state of oversupply most of the time, thus depressing prices. Even if that were not true, what is true is that most commodity markets in the postwar period have more often been in a state of oversupply than undersupply, and that in the periods of undersupply, the lessons of history have been ignored and capacity increased, thus leading to oversupply.

These market fluctuations generally favor the buyer and thus have put continuous pressure upon the commodities account manager. This pressure has been especially severe when the account managers in Japan do not reside in the country, for they are ignorant of local market trends, have superficial personal relationships with Japanese clients, and are insensitive to Japanese business culture.

The biggest criticism leveled at such account managers has been their failure to establish representative offices in Tokyo, relying instead on their trade ministry's Tokyo office for current data. To do this is to blatantly ignore the human side of business in Japan. For instance, a Japanese minerals negotiator told me of a visiting account manager who had communicated acceptance of the Japanese offer by telephoning late at night. Not being able to find the Japanese negotiator, he gave the message of acceptance to a junior, a shocking and unbelievable display of bad business manners in Japan. In another case, when the Japanese side tabled a new proposal for a billion-dollar contract for discussion, the visitor's sole reaction was to discuss how many copies and what kind of printing he wanted in the final contract.

Liaison offices in Tokyo represent some improvement over the visiting account manager, but the real advances only come when a full sales and marketing organization—as with Neuerbach or Calco—is set up in Japan.

CONCLUSION

To be a successful negotiator, one really needs, first, to live in and understand the market that one is dealing with, not only from one's own viewpoint, but also from that of the other side. Second, it is important to understand the culture and how local people usually negotiate with or influence one another. Finally, success in negotiation does not evolve from having fixed ideas about the culture or its people, for ultimately every company you deal with, and every individual buyer from that company, is unique. You have to relate to that person, not to a stereotype that could lead you to treat all Japanese or other nationals as though they are all the same. If you recognize this, and, in addition, always come into any negotiation better prepared than the other side, you are probably a professional negotiator already.

Ongoing relationships between Japanese and their foreign associates show both mutual obligation and willingness to compromise (typical of gamelike negotiation) along with small everyday frictions, uncertainties, and suspicions. Calco's Midway and Neuerbach's Dewey—one a professional manager and expert negotiator, the other a linguist, Japan specialist, and latter-day businessman—each show intelligence, sensitivity, prudence, and strategic sense as they take charge of regular business negotiations with the Japanese. There is an instructive contrast with Gordon Hathaway, who is younger, less experienced, and/or less knowledgeable about Japan. Hathaway seems to feel that his business life in Tokyo is a constant struggle for survival, probably more difficult than for Midway or Dewey, for, unlike them, Hathaway does not represent a big manufacturer but (the Japanese would perceive) is a "mere" broker, and so is entitled to rather less respect.

In conclusion, we can see that there is a wide variety of possible friendly negotiations with the Japanese, and that the ongoing relationship has to be continuously managed like any other. Each negotiator and each occasion of contact should be specifically prepared for, each case treated on its merits, if friendly relationships—and a game-type atmosphere—are to be maintained. Most of the cases in this chapter reveal occasions of potential conflict, but the imperatives of the underlying relationships, plus the skills of individual managers, were the key factors in resolving conflict and restoring balance. The activities, skills, and know-how of the professional managers featured here also show what scarcely needs to be asserted: that there is no place in international negotiations with the Japanese for the John Wayne-type, shoot-from-the-hip, "wing it" bargainers.

INEFFECTIVE NEGOTIATION
WITH
THE JAPANESE

Chapter 5

The Roots of Conflict

In Chapter 2, I suggested that it is useful to think of two polar sorts of negotiation—game-type negotiation, which is competitive but bound by certain rules, and tactical negotiation, where all rules break down and the actors behave in unexpected, unprecedented, and disturbing ways. When negotiation leaders are effective managers, such flare-ups can be quickly quelled, but when the spokesmen are less effective, as in the following set of cases, negotiations tend toward the tactical, with the actors beginning to feel more remote, to see each other as more alien, incomprehensible, untrustworthy, and unidentifiable with. If stereotypes are relied on to explain why the other side is behaving so "offensively" or "unethically," then the common interests that brought them to the meeting in the first place will cease to be motivating, and all productive negotiation of business will cease.

The sources of conflict in cross-cultural negotiation are diverse, but the most common are due to problems of communication. These include misunderstandings, either because of intermediaries such as interpreters or because of the actors themselves. Misunderstandings arise in many ways, however. A strong expression of emotion by one side may *appear* as hostility to the other side when it might only be an expression of confusion. Or some ways of behavior may give offense where none was intended through the violation of cultural norms of which the person was unaware.

Furthermore, even the simplest language can be a potential source of misunderstanding. For instance, the word "negotiation" and its usual translation "*kōshō*" have significantly different meanings. "*Kōshō*" has nuances in Japanese of fighting, conflict, strategy (*senryaku*), and verbal debate (*iiau*), whereas "negotiation" lacks these overtones and usually suggests discussion, concession, and conference. This is not just an academic point because businessmen who think of negotiation as *kōshō* or *iiau* will, not surprisingly, enter the meeting with a more aggressive intent than those who view it as "negotiation."

So even in the beginning there may be some difference in the feelings we have about the negotiation. I see this in the negotiation trainings I conduct in Japan. In English they are called "Seminars for strengthening international negotiation skills"; in Japanese this is rendered as "*Kōshōryoku o kyōchō suru seminā.*" This is an adequate literal translation of the English, but the aggressive implication of "*kōshō*" still remains. Consequently, there are always some Japanese in the seminars who at the beginning believe that I will tell them how to "fight" Westerners better, and it takes a little time for them to discover that this is not the approach I am offering.

Actually, I believe that the "fight" interpretation of negotiation is held by many Japanese businessmen vis-à-vis Westerners. They have developed this concept as an emotional reaction to years of experience of Western argumentativeness and verbal aggression. We have seen the tip of that iceberg in the case of the two broadcasting organizations. Thus, Japanese frequently enter negotiations expecting to be given a hard time, so they must arm themselves in advance. And if they happen to have the greater bargaining power (i.e., buyers in a buyers' market, or sellers in a sellers' market), their armory is likely to include unconcealed arrogance, unless the foreign side disarms them with a deferential, unargumentative approach.

It is possible to conclude that Western arrogance and aggression over the years is now reaping a harvest of distorted perceptions and stereotypes. But what is certain is that international negotiations are very stressful on individual negotiators and their team members. You must be careful what you say to people who are not on your team in public and in private. You have to monitor your speech, otherwise you cannot be sure what you will reveal. In my view, the Japanese are far better at this than Americans or Europeans because their everyday behavior consists of such verbal restraint and selectivity. Therefore, relatively speaking, negotiation stress of this kind is more intense for Westerners, and there is greater likelihood of them losing control and showing verbal aggression or making impulsive counteroffers.

There is support for this idea in research I have done on Japanese–Western interpersonal communication. The Japanese say they have "complexes" about Westerners, that they feel awkward and uncomfortable when talking to them. Concurrently, there is a widespread belief in Japan that Westerners are more relaxed, more expressive communicators who are at home with the Japanese and other peoples. My own research doesn't support this. In fact, Westerners much more often say they have the following problems with Japanese: "Difficult to understand how they think, so I feel awkward"; "Difficult to understand the personality of individual Japanese"; "Feel uncomfortable with Japanese who behave formally."

In contrast, these are not problems with the Japanese. The main problems for them are: "Appreciating the impact of my behavior on Western clients"; "Using English effectively with correct pauses and word emphasis."

While the Japanese have language problems, it is the Westerners who more often have feelings of being unable to read the Japanese, of awkwardness and discomfort. If this is so, it is easy to understand why Westerners should lose their composure or feel intimidated when facing the Japanese, and end up without concluding a satisfactory agreement.

There are a number of other reasons why negotiating with the Japanese can be singularly trying. Before presenting the cases in this section, here is a representative sample of those problems:

Misunderstandings: These can stem from language inadequacies on one or both sides. Many Americans believe that the Japanese who speaks passable conversational English can comprehend colloquial expressions, jokes, and even topical small talk, but this is rarely true. The problem is not just language, for such stories may demand a grounding in the everyday culture or current affairs of your country that the Japanese (or any other foreigner) do not possess.

Tactics Backfire: The use of obvious tactics is frowned upon by most Japanese as distasteful and low-class. In response, they may simply smile, with a little condescension, and indicate that they recognize your game but are not going to play it. On the other hand, the Japanese have a whole range of special tactics that they feel no qualms about using but which they do not normally class as tactics. This is a subject treated later in the book.

Secretiveness: The Japanese are more secretive than most people you will encounter. They will reveal little of their game plan at the beginning, or indicate who their real decision-makers are.

Lack of Details: The Japanese are not accustomed to negotiating a contract or relationship in an item-by-item way. Usually, they seek a broad agreement first.

Misreading Your Opposite Number: The polite, soft-spoken,

Japanese you initially face is rarely susceptible to intimidation. In difficult negotiations, for instance, he may simply refuse to accept your agenda or your order of topics, or he may resort to silence if your side tries to intimidate or rile him. He will not try to debate with you or better you verbally.

Excellent Teamwork: The Japanese work as a cohesive team, under one spokesman, and the chances of having other team members express individual views, especially differing views, are essentially nonexistent. Part of the reason for this is that the Japanese spokesman is almost never the key decision-maker, and the key decision-maker (usually a company director) will almost certainly not be present in the negotiating room until the Japanese side is convinced that it wants to reach agreement with you. Again, the cohesiveness of the team shows up especially when a Western team becomes aggressive, with many people speaking and making demands of the Japanese. This area of cohesive teamwork is the greatest strength in Japanese international negotiation, and the lack of it the greatest single weakness of Western teams.

No Feedback: The Japanese do not applaud clever arguments, rarely acknowledge your key points, never give praise, and generally give little feedback. You may be asked to repeat your story to a number of different people. This takes the persuasive edge off many presentations, especially because often there is no nonverbal feedback, such as a nod or smile, to acknowledge your messages.

Most of the above observations apply especially to Japanese managers in major companies. However, according to both my own experiences as a negotiator in Japan and research I have done in Southeast Asian countries, the small-scale Japanese businessman or trader, as opposed to those working for large corporations, is a rather different species. He may be highly tactical and secretive, always trying to gain control of the situation by asking questions but not answering any, resisting a personal relationship, or being superficially friendly but personally cold. Southeast Asians contrast the Japanese trader unfavorably with local or Western merchant counterparts, and my own experience is somewhat consistent with this. Small businesses in Japan still retain many feudal elements in human relations, with managers favoring a coercive, authoritarian style that contrasts greatly with the more democratic, open style of the well-educated senior managers in leading Japanese companies.

The cases that now follow illustrate problems that can arise from many of the difficulties cited above.

CASE STUDY: A LICENSING AGREEMENT DISPUTE

Key Points

The Japanese can be emotional in ways that Westerners may be unprepared for and can be easily offended by some Westerners, even when no offense was intended.

The American legalistic or lecturing style of behavior is offensive to many Japanese.

The Japanese expect people younger than them, and/or of lower status, to be deferential, and will be annoyed if they are not.

Verbosity is seen as a personal defect in Japan. Verbose people, lacking in sensitivity or readiness to listen to others, are not appropriate as negotiators, however senior they happen to be in the organization.

The Japanese handle every business problem on a face-to-face basis, not by telephone or by mail.

Communication in English to the Japanese should be carefully planned—interpreters used, language simplified, presentation points and order thoroughly prepared in advance, visual aids used, and ample time allowed for questions.

Frankness and honesty in the face of problems, and a

readiness to apologize for mistakes, unintentional offense, or rudeness can clear the air quickly with the Japanese.

*Even the bitterest conflicts with the Japanese are resolvable if we can develop a comprehensive understanding of their needs, perceptions, and feelings.

*Every group negotiating a complex or sensitive issue with the Japanese can benefit from the inclusion of someone with deep cultural insights and strong intuitive power.

After a comprehensive investigation of the Japanese market, Rod R. Murray, international director of Warner Foods Corporation, a Fortune 500 company, approached each of Japan's leading food manufacturers to sound out interest in working with Warner. Natsuyama K.K., one of the five largest food manufacturers in Japan, was most interested in developing a long-term relationship with Warner. In March 1982, detailed discussions were held between Murray and Jiro Yamashita, international director and later president of Natsuyama. This led to a memorandum of understanding between the two managements and to a twelve-year contract for the exclusive agency and licensing rights for the local manufacture of Warner products in Japan by Natsuyama. This agreement was concluded with Natsuyama in early September 1982, and in November 1982 the first products were shipped from Warner to Natsuyama. In January 1984, Natsuyama commenced local manufacture and marketing of their first Warner product, Warner Cheese Dessert, in plastic containers. At the same time, however, Natsuyama continued to import the canned Warner Cheese Dessert, marketing it through the same channels, for those who preferred the foreign product.

Whatever the reasons, by the end of 1984, sales of the locally produced cheese dessert had fallen well below the level expected when the agreement was signed. This meant that under the provisions of the licensing contract, a minimum royalty (i.e., a fixed amount to be paid when sales fell below a specified minimum, replacing the royalty percentage) on the local manufacture of Warner Cheese Dessert was to be paid to Warner Foods. In early March 1985, Murray wrote to Natsuyama indicating that although royalties had been remitted to Warner based on the volume sold, they had not yet remitted the balance of the royalty payment owed Warner in accordance with the minimum royalty provision in the agreement.

Natsuyama began contesting the "fairness" of the minimum royalty payment they were obliged to pay under the terms of the licensing agreement. In particular, Natsuyama argued that local manufacture could only be said to have begun when the locally made product in plastic containers had substantially replaced the imports. Since, they argued, four-fifths of overall product sales in Japan for 1984 were imports, local production could not be said to have begun, and therefore minimum royalties did not apply.

In fact, Natsuyama felt that it was being victimized. The sales of the imported canned product were apparently inhibiting sales of the local product in plastic containers, and some senior Natsuyama managers felt that Warner Foods, through the minimum royalty clause, was squeezing "double profit" (minimum royalties on the local product plus export profits on the foreign product), while Natsuyama was "losing money" on their local cheese dessert manufacturing.

The president, Jiro Yamashita, felt particularly indignant toward Murray, seeing him as the person responsible for trying to squeeze Natsuyama. For a time, Yamashita left the negotiations to his subordinates, only to find that when he was out of the country, they had met with key Warner people and agreed to pay the full amount outstanding according to the minimum royalty formula.

Infuriated, Yamashita and his lawyers framed a letter in English to Edgar Masters, chairman of Warner, setting out the Natsuyama position essentially as given above, a position which other Natsuyama staff had not apparently been able to appreciate since they had agreed almost without argument to pay the outstanding amount. This letter requested the chairman of Warner to "reconsider the issues involved, which may include return of the remittance" of the minimum royalty made by junior Natsuyama staff three weeks earlier. There were also other requests to Warner Foods that, in the context of the dispute, actually made the Warner people more wary and suspicious of Natsuyama's real intentions.

The letter from Yamashita troubled Masters and all the Warner staff involved. Its tone clearly indicated that Yamashita wanted to deal not with Murray, the international director, but with Masters himself. That was out of the question for Masters, who fully trusted Murray.

Eventually, it was Murray who replied to Yamashita, beginning by saying that he had been asked to do so by Masters. Unfortunately, it became a typical Murray letter—long, excessively detailed, legalistically toned—which angered Yamashita even further. But the Warner people were not to have any hint of this for some months. During that period, Murray wrote to Kishi, the marketing manager of Natsuyama (who reported to Yamashita), making new proposals for the calculation of royalties and for the redefinition of some ambiguous terms in the licensing agreement, and requesting long-delayed discussion on the marketing of other Warner products that had been successful in other countries. These proposals became the basis for a meeting in Tokyo in August 1985, attended by Murray and three of his corporate staff, and Yamashita, Kishi, and four of their staff.

Murray felt he had prepared carefully for this meeting, incurring the substantial expense of bringing three of his staff to Tokyo especially for it. Unfortunately, it was a disaster. Whatever the Western side proposed, Yamashita blocked, criticized, or vetoed. Early in the meeting, moreover, in commenting on the Warner approach to royalty payments, Yamashita straightfacedly said, "You are nothing but a bunch of bloodsucking shylocks masquerading under a repulsive veneer of virtue." Murray and his colleagues merely smiled wanly, believing it to be no more than a weak attempt at humor. Three and a half hours into the same meeting, a now clearly angry Yamashita repeated the line, this time adding, for good measure, that the Warner people had done nothing but try to "trick, lie, and cheat" Natsuyama. This time the Westerners did not treat it lightly.

"It was a savage, unconscionable statement," Murray was to say later, "the like of which I have never heard in any business meeting anywhere, and Japan is the last place in the world I would ever have expected to have heard it. It left all of us in shock, overwhelmed and speechless at Yamashita's language and the near bankruptcy of the relationship."

The Warner people now felt that the relationship was in its dying stages, even though they had no real knowledge of what had led to Yamashita's outburst. Informally, they sounded out junior Natsuyama staff to discover what had gone wrong. They learned little. Their confidence shattered, they floated two other ideas: first, to use a "go-between" to help mutual understanding and develop strategies to resolve the situation; second, to negotiate "a dissolution of the entire relationship."

Three months after that devastating meeting, Warner Foods still had no answers to their dilemma, no firm strategies, no understanding of the Japanese. In another two weeks, they would attend another meeting with Natsuyama, without a single trump card in their hand. The one bright note had been another letter from Yamashita to Edgar Masters, which proposed an alternative definition of the minimum royalty calculation. The tone of that letter suggested that Natsuyama did want to continue the relationship, but at that stage it just seemed like one more inconsistent piece added to the jigsaw puzzle of their relationship.

At this point, Warner retained a Western negotiation consultant to advise it on the forthcoming meeting. After reviewing documents covering the entire project and interviewing Murray at length by telephone, the consultant made a series of observations that included the following:

1. Yamashita's behavior seemed calculated, deliberate, and had given him the initiative, the "moral vantage point," in the negotiations;

2. Yamashita probably had some personal animus against Murray that was feeding the flames of dispute;

3. Reasons for this might lie in Murray's letters, which were verbose, legalistic, and lecture-ish, and, though not difficult to understand, were likely to be culturally offensive to the Japanese. Also important was the fact that Murray always relied on correspondence, rather than face-to-face discussion or even consultation by telephone, to handle problems, which projected a cold impression to the Japanese;

4. Yamashita considered his social/business status to be substantially higher than that of Murray. Hence, he never replied to Murray's letters and felt justified in talking down to Murray (culturally acceptable in Japan).

The consultant recommended the following:

1. Change your entire communication style. Do not rely on written communications but deal face-to-face on awkward issues. In future meetings, use well-briefed, professional interpreters (not a bilingual member of the Natsuyama company as had previously been done).

2. Before entering into substantive negotiation with Natsuyama, undertake a complete review of your own corporate needs and goals in Japan, make an objective appraisal of how well you have handled the relationship so far and whether you can handle it in the future in ways that will meet your corporate needs.

3. Since you are already thinking of abandoning the con-

nection, take strength from that to negotiate a relationship that is more likely to work, one based on sound human relations.

4. Commit yourselves to make an open-ended investment of time to get it right in Japan.

Moreover, the consultant strongly recommended that Warner begin the next session with Natsuyama by first making a well-planned comprehensive presentation of the negotiation background and current situation in the following order: the impact of the current international environment; Japan–U.S. relations; the international business environment; a statement of the history of the project; what it hopes to achieve; what it believes Natsuyama hopes to achieve; what has actually been achieved; how it views the problems in the current situation; to admit frankly where it felt things had gone wrong, or where it misunderstood the Natsuyama side; the negotiable and non-negotiable items, especially its proposals in the fields of marketing, accountability, royalties, overall management of the relationship and of Warner's business in Japan. A statement should be made of the fresh resolve to manage (i.e., continuously negotiate) the Natsuyama relationship in the future, rather than rely too heavily upon occasional, ad hoc interpretations of the contract.

The consultant added, "Recognize that this may be your only opportunity to make such a comprehensive statement of your position since you will quickly get into detailed discussions, where it is inevitable that perspective will be lost or greatly diminished."

Murray and his three Warner colleagues arrived in Tokyo on December 2, 1985, very much in two minds about the forthcoming negotiation with the Natsuyama group. They met with the consultant and a professional interpreter on the following day to review their approach and do whatever rehearsal was necessary. The negotiation was to begin on December 4.

In the pre-negotiation meeting, the consultant was given full freedom to orchestrate the organization of the team, as well as the behavior of individual members, in a way reminiscent of a theatrical director. The points he stressed were:

1. Before the negotiation began, Warner should develop the agenda items and agenda order it wanted, and send its regional representative who had the best relationship with the Natsuyama people to negotiate this. In particular, he urged the Warner team to try to get the long-delayed topic of new product marketing included in the agreed agenda.
2. Warner should make the opening presentation as comprehensive and fair as possible.
3. Warner should make the presentation in point form, with each point pre-printed on flip-charts. After making a point and clarifying it, the spokesman (Murray) was to stop and allow time for interpretation and for questions. The increased time required to present the complete Warner case would, he said, be more than compensated for by the communication clarity that would be achieved. He suggested that Warner should resist temptations to embroider, ad lib, or add new points, and should stick to the script.
4. Each member of the Western team was assigned a specific role. One was to be assistant to the spokesman, monitoring all in-coming messages (especially from their own team members), thereby reducing the information-processing load on the spokesman when he needed his full powers of concentration on the job at hand. The other two were briefed to observe the nonverbal behavior of the Japanese, especially after their spokesman made key points or new offers. The consultant gave examples of the kind of nonverbal behavior to watch for, especially behavior that might signal interest, approval, or resistance.

5. At all times, members were to show strong nonverbal support of points made by their leader. They were to nod approvingly and supportively as he made each point, looking first at him and then at the Japanese side.

How the Negotiation Fared: The regional representative met with his Japanese counterpart on the afternoon of December 3 to negotiate the agenda. He obtained agreement on all items except for new product marketing, since the Japanese said his bosses were absolutely against this point being discussed at that time. This was something of a set-back to Warner.

The next day, the meeting went according to plan. After the usual greetings and small talk, Murray asked for and was given permission to review the relationship to date. After twenty minutes, it became clear to the Western side that the Natsuyama people were showing a high degree of interest, approval, and cordiality in response to Murray's points, especially those dealing with his own reflections on his past performance as a communicator. Toward the end of his presentation, Murray mentioned that he would have liked to discuss the issue of new product marketing, but he appreciated that it was something that Natsuyama did not want to discuss at that time. He was about to continue when Yamashita interrupted him, almost apologetically, and began to explain why he had not wanted to include that item. This was, he said, essentially a statement about internal Natsuyama problems, financial constraints, and competing priorities, the first statement of its kind that Natsuyama had ever made to Warner. Ironically, it contained all the information that Murray had wanted to gain from a discussion of the topic.

The overflow of frankness and honesty on both sides signaled a startling change in the personal feelings of people on both sides. Murray's eyes began to glisten, Yamashita softened his haughtiness, and his lieutenants were beaming openly. The Westerners took a little longer to catch on, but they, too, realized it. "By God, we've done it! We've finally broken through the log-jam of distorted perceptions and accumulated misunderstanding!" was how one Warner executive expressed his feelings at the time.

Comments

Natsuyama and Warner, unsurprisingly, did not live happily ever after this, but they did come out of the meeting with mutual respect restored, and with the feeling they had put their views clearly, been listened to, and their differences of view had been respected.

Natsuyama did reconsider the new product ideas put forward by Warner and decided, to Warner's delight, to proceed in a limited way with the most promising new product. Murray came to recognize that his communication style was not effective with the Japanese, so he gave greater responsibility for intercompany communications to his marketing director. Yamashita remained prickly and aloof, though he kept in the background more. However, when the royalty issue was in its final stages of resolution, he appeared once more, telling his subordinates that before Natsuyama would finally agree, he wanted a written apology from Warner for how it had treated Natsuyama on the minimum royalty issue. Murray did not take that lightly, although a formal letter of regret was finally devised that satisfied both men, and so closed one chapter in the saga.

CASE STUDY: THE THREE-BILLION-DOLLAR SUGAR DISPUTE

Key Points

Long-term contracts with the Japanese suffer, in Western eyes, from the Japanese refusal to honor the contract when circumstances change.

Japanese have a tendency to persist with extreme strategies even if they believe that there is no hope of winning.

Japanese quickly come to resent those who refuse to accede to requests for help in times of trouble.

The lack of respect for abstract principles and the law makes it easy for some Japanese to break contracts that have become "inconvenient."

In 1977, after twelve months of fruitless negotiation with Australia on lowering the price of sugar in a long-term, $3-billion contract, Japanese sugar refiners shocked the world by refusing to accept any more Australian shipments. By the end of the dispute, some 30 ships, carrying over 200,000 tons of sugar (then valued at $50,000,000) were riding at anchor off Yokohama, waiting for the Japanese to accept the sugar, and some ships were there for as long as three months. Japan's international reputation sank to a low ebb as it was castigated by countries all over the world as immoral and unethical for its refusal to honor a contract it had entered into with open eyes.

The original Japan–Australia Long-Term Sugar Agreement was signed in December 1974, after seven months of negotiation. CSR Ltd., the sugar agent for the Queensland government, concluded it during a year of unstable sugar supplies and escalating prices resulting from the oil crisis of November 1973, the collapse of international sugar agreements, and poor harvests, especially in Cuba. Prices in 1974 shot up from a low of $143 to $650 per ton in October. In this contract, Australia sought to stabilize its sugar industry by offering long-term contracts (LTCs), and the first nation approached, in April 1974, was Japan. After one month of negotiations, however, the Japanese requested a suspension. Their aim was to see what offers they could get from other countries.

By a process of elimination, Japan found that only Australia was in a position to enter into an LTC. According to some Japanese refiners, the Australians had used coercion, saying in effect that "If you, Japan, do not conclude an LTC with us, we cannot guarantee to supply you with anywhere near the quantity we have in the past." The Australians deny this, saying that all the refiners wanted was the relatively low-cost Australian sugar. Moreover, in 1974, sugar sales by Australia to Japan dropped (were cut, some Japanese say) from 600,000 tons to 230,000 tons.

The eventual contract covered a period of five years beginning in 1975, with 600,000 tons per year, half of it calculated at A$405 per ton, and half at US$525 per ton (or an average of £229 sterling).

The LTC was supported by an exchange of letters between the two governments concerned, apparently to the effect that neither side would take discriminatory steps to restrict imports or exports, or impose tariff barriers. Nothing official, however, has ever been published on the content of the letters.

The London daily price (LPD) at time of the LTC signing was around £400 per ton. The Mitsui and Mitsubishi trading companies signed the contract on behalf of the thirty-three Japanese sugar refiners and arranged for some refiners to take a greater share of the LTC sugar than their current market share. The subsequent decline in world sugar prices was to cause those refiners with a higher ratio of LTC fixed price sugar to go much deeper into the red.

The Japanese sugar refining industry may not have been as jubilant over the LTC as the Japanese Ministry of Agriculture, Forestry and Fisheries (MAF) and some sections of the press. Some said the refiners had been worried about the real possibility of a price decline, while an editorial in the *Nihon Keizai Shimbun* (a conservative business daily) of December 19, 1974, reflecting industry opinion, cautioned that "international sugar prices could decline sharply."

Problems arose almost immediately. By July 1975, the world price declined to £130 (compared to the LTC price of £229). In Japan, domestic demand was stagnant, and sugar stockpiled. Two requests were made in 1975 to have shipments deferred, and 90,000 tons were deferred until the first half of 1976, but these were only stop-gap measures and did not solve the problems of high and growing Japanese inventories, stagnant demand, unprofitable trading, and escalating deficits. The Japanese wanted the LTC reviewed in line with a clause that said: "Both contractors shall reexamine the operation and continuity of this contract at least once a year."

The Japanese required substantial changes, especially in price, which they believed fell within this Review Clause. An English contract lawyer was retained in July 1976 to advise them, after a request to CSR for a price reduction.

The Australians replied four months later with news of an impending ministerial mission to Japan. Called the Sullivan Mission (after its leader, the Queensland Minister for Primary Industries), it arrived in Japan in January for on-the-spot investigations. From these the Australians prepared their tactics, which were to insist that: 1. A full two years of the LTC should be completed before a price review would be agreed to; 2. A rationalization of the Japanese sugar refining industry should be undertaken; 3. Sugar import duty and commodity tax should be reduced; 4. Once a new LTC was negotiated, no further demands would be made by the Japanese for a price revision.

When these demands were put to the Japanese, they were shocked and resentful. It was a purely commercial arrangement, they argued, and matters such as industry rationalization or tax reductions were unrelated and concerned their own government. MAF agreed. In this context, the opening negotiations were unproductive.

The following four months saw little progress. To assist the cash flow position of the refiners, the Australians proposed a stepped price scheme, allowing for reduced payments in the first two years, compensated for by higher payments later, but this was rejected as a token reduction. In May, the Japanese made their first price offer of £160 a ton, or £40 above the current world price, but £69 below the LTC price. This encouraged the Australians for a short time, but continuous negotiations through June failed to move the parties any closer.

The Japanese, on the advice of their English legal counsel, then began to threaten to refuse accepting further shipments. The Australians responded with a revised price offer of £200 as their "final non-negotiable offer." The Japanese rejected this, and formally told CSR that it was in breach of contract (for failing to observe the Review Clause), that the LTC was therefore terminated, and that all further shipments would be rejected.

Rejection of the LTC by the Japanese meant that sugar began to accumulate off Yokohama Port, totaling 213,000 tons by the time of the resolution of the dispute. It was a permanent and profound embarrassment to the Japanese throughout this period.

Equally disturbing was the political pressure exercised upon Japan by the Australian government. This lead to the active involvement of the Fukuda Cabinet in the dispute (from the end of August), which sent directives to MAF to make recommendations for a speedy resolution. This led to: 1. The exercise of administrative guidance by MAF to the refiners in the search for a rational solution to the problem, especially to the vexed question of accepting a fixed price for any extension of the contract; 2. The development by MAF of a new law to rationalize the sugar refining industry.

After final haggling, and last-ditch resistance to any concession by one refiner, a new contract was agreed to on October 13, 1977.

The new LTC represented an extension of two years with a variable price component. Due to the rapid strengthening of the yen that began in September 1977, the real price to the Japanese had dropped some 20 percent, while a further 7 percent reduction came from the revised Australian price offer that the Japanese finally accepted.

While the Japanese refiners came out of the negotiations better off than they had feared, there was some residual bitterness against CSR, both among the Japanese refiners and, interestingly, among ministers of the Queensland government. CSR immediately transferred some senior staff out of their sugar department, probably at the request of the Queensland government.

Why was the original LTC ever signed? The sugar LTC was concluded at a time of worldwide economic uncertainty and, in Japan, panic. If, as one authority has written, the Japanese were prone to agree to contracts "that foreigners have improvidentially insisted upon, when deep down they know they cannot live with them," how much more must this have been the case during the original negotiations in 1974. CSR people frequently boasted about their "supreme intelligence effort" in negotiating the original contract, but they did not seem to have questioned whether, given traditional Japanese attitudes to contracts plus the volatility of world sugar prices, the LTC should ever have been pursued by the Australians at all. Indeed, the CSR people repeatedly told the press that they knew how risky the LTC was when it was signed. If they did, in fact, recognize that there could not be the necessary mutuality for a secure contract in the Western sense, it is mystifying why they concluded it. Until the actors on each side drop their excessive secretiveness, we are unlikely to know the real story.

The role of the mass media in each country, and in other countries interested in the sugar negotiations, is strikingly different. When we consider Japan's domestic media (newspapers and magazines), the reporting of the sugar dispute from both Australian and Japanese sources in the two countries was extremely comprehensive and mostly even-handed, giving insight into both points of view. On the other hand, reporting in Australia was more limited, with most of the news emanating from Australian sources in Japan or Australia. One reason for the bias was the system of "press clubs" in Japan. Ministries, companies, and organizations who regularly make press statements or give briefings, did so to a select group of press club reporters, the others not being admitted. During the sugar dispute, no foreign correspondents in Japan were invited to any ministry or company briefings, and the little news that they were able to report from Japanese sources was essentially in the form of hand-outs from friendly Japanese reporters.

There was also a difference in reporting style, with the Australians preoccupied with the "immorality" of the Japanese breach of contract. In contrast, the Japanese press, which presented the underlying problems on both sides, reflected a more complex set of attitudes toward big business in Japan, as well as a genuine cultural difference. The Japanese are prone to personalize relationships and to desire outcomes that are mutually satisfying rather than those determined by impersonal principles.

There seems little doubt that foreign opinions about the sugar dispute were substantially determined by the "bad press" emanating from non-Japanese sources. Of course, the dishonoring of the contract was hardly defensible; it met with severe criticism even within Japan, and only one newspaper, the *Nihon Keizai Shimbun*, consistently defended the refiners' refusal to accept the contracted sugar.

The Japanese government directly intervened in the dispute, via the MAF, which "guided" the sugar refiners' proposals, particularly in the last two months of the dispute, and drafted the bill that permitted industry restructuring. In addition, the Ministry for International Trade and Industry (MITI) was represented in all consultations because of its responsibilities in international trade. MITI officials tended to be privately critical of MAF and the sugar refiners' "intransigence" over the LTC and of their insularity.

The Japanese Ministry of Foreign Affairs was also a concerned party. Although not involved in the negotiations, its embassy and consulates in Australia were briefed both by the ministry in Tokyo and by all the Japanese who visited Australia in connection with the dispute, such as MAF officials, sugar refiners, or trading company executives. Japanese diplomats in Australia provided Tokyo with continuous analyses of the Australian sugar industry, but there is good reason to believe that that information probably never went beyond the Foreign Ministry in Tokyo, and certainly did not get to the sugar refiners.

On the Australian side, the Sugar Board, CSR, and the Queensland government all relied entirely upon the Commonwealth government for the exercise of high-level influence and for general intelligence. In particular, CSR negotiators in Tokyo had immediate access to the daily news translation service of the Australian Embassy. In addition, the Australian commercial minister and his staff provided general support and were the communication (telex) link between Australia and the CSR negotiators.

Although the CSR people, in their criticisms of the Japanese press, complained about the problems of what they called the 4 Ms ("misunderstanding, mistranslation, misinformation, and misinterpretation"), none in the CSR team spoke any Japanese, nor was an interpreter used in the negotiations. However, an interpreter was hired for occasional press briefings, which may have been the source of the irritation over the 4 Ms. The problems that occurred might have been avoided or minimized by more effective use and prior briefing of an interpreter who had good background knowledge of the issues.

On the Japanese side, the refiners were mistaken in their analysis of the actual identity of the key Australian decision-makers. They wrongly assumed that the Queensland Minister for Primary Industries was the central decision-maker, and ignored the crucial role of the chairman of the Sugar Board. In this, they overstressed the effect of political factors on Australian negotiating moves. They would have been better informed if they had established direct lines of communication with the Foreign Ministry, or, better still, with the Japanese Consulate in Brisbane, Queensland.

Comments

Tactically speaking, the Japanese refiners' approach to the negotiations was a limited one. This was due partly to their being the initiator of the dispute, and partly to a clear disinterest in or lack of appreciation or understanding of the possible benefits to be gained from the flexible use of tactics.

As the initiator of the dispute, the Japanese were seen as the aggressor. In the first few months, however, and certainly until March 1977, they did not behave as aggressors might. Leaks to the press of points critical of or detrimental to the other side were rare while, within the negotiations, neither side began any hard bargaining until April 1977. Until that date the Japanese posture would have to be described as "low," because they continued to believe that the Australians would accept their view that the Review Clause could entail a price review.

When it became clear that the Australians were not going to accept the Japanese interpretation of the Review Clause but were going to insist that the first two years of the LTC be completed before commencing any serious negotiations, and were not in any case going to offer more than a 5 percent to 7 percent price reduction, the refiners chose to make the following moves—to increase their offer to £160 and, when this failed, to cancel the LTC and reject the sugar.

While the latter move is clearly aggressive, it is also plausible to view the refiners' prior behavior as long-suffering, so that, as the third year approached with no solution in sight, there may have been no time left for the use of a tactic other than rejection. If so, then the Japanese can be said to have persevered, more than in retrospect seemed wise, with a policy of reasonableness in negotiation, when the Australians from the beginning were determined to give very little and to take as much time as was necessary to achieve their goals.

If the refiners had anticipated the inflexible Australian stance, they would have been able to exploit one or both of two tactics. They could have used the mass media in both countries to emphasize their view of the Review Clause and to accuse the Australians, by implication, of not honoring the spirit of the LTC. That might have put Australia on the defensive and perhaps generated some sorely needed international sympathy for Japan. A second possible tactic could have been to attack a repeated Australian claim that its sugar industry had made an investment of A$300–$400 million on the basis of the LTC with Japan.

The development of a hardened Japanese response to Australian inflexibility was in part delayed by use of a number of Australian tactics. For instance, the CSR negotiators claimed several times that negotiations would have to be deferred or that new offers could not be made due to circumstances beyond their control, for example, a strike by Japanese sugar industry workers or a forthcoming conference of Australian cane growers. The refiners not only had an unrealistic appreciation of the CSR negotiators' intentions in respect to changing the LTC, they also overestimated their power. They assumed for many months that the negotiators were given considerable discretion in negotiation, and it was only much later that they gave thought to alternative hypotheses about decision-making on the Australian side.

Most of all, however, the Australian planned tactic was to wait for the intervention of the Japanese government via administrative guidance and promised industry reform. That ultimate intervention can be attributed to two concurrent circumstances. One was the intense political pressure exerted upon Japan by the Australian and Queensland governments, by the Australian and overseas press, and, indirectly, by diplomatic pressure from other countries. The other was the progressive build-up of 213,000 tons of sugar at Yokohama, surely the critical factor.

In summary, the differences between the two parties can be described thus. The Australians were strategically well prepared. They had anticipated the need for information, time, and had devised strong opening moves. All of this was in expectation of something analogous to guerrilla warfare. On the other hand, the Japanese were not prepared for nor were they anticipating "war" in the Australian sense, believing it incompatible with customer–buyer relations. Escalation of the dispute might have been minimized had different individuals been in the CSR negotiation team. At any rate, those who would likewise confront Japan may have learned that one tactic above all works with the Japanese, namely, long and sustained pressure from the outside until the government is compelled to act.

THE JAPANESE STYLE OF CONFLICT ESCALATION

As the sugar dispute demonstrates, one cultural tendency of Japanese who are in trouble is to throw themselves on the mercy of the other party, in confident expectation of assistance and support. That, of course, is the essence of the *naniwabushi* approach described in Chapter 1, which was well demonstrated in the early stages of the sugar dispute. But this expectation is rarely met when the other party is foreign. So if *naniwabushi* fails, what can we expect as the next Japanese step?

If it is a domestic negotiation, and the petitioner is a more powerful company, thinly veiled threats of "commercial ostracism" are not uncommon. Certainly the threat of litigation, or actually beginning litigation, is the exception.

In international negotiation, there are more varied strategies, not unexpectedly, since the international world of business is much more loosely structured and much less interdependent than in Japan. Suzuki's diplomacy in the Toyosan case in Chapter 2 is one style. Bearing in mind his personality, and the fact that the British owned 51 percent of the venture, the only real option open to Suzuki, had he failed to persuade the British, was to continue to keep plugging away.

Given different personalities, different priorities, and higher economic risks, patience is much less likely. In one of Japan's largest annual commercial negotiations (running into several billion dollars), the Japanese side one year insisted that, due to slackening demand and increasing inventories, there was no way it could meet the foreign side's price. The foreigners, however, held their ground stubbornly. After many fruitless meetings, the Japanese team leader eventually exploded at the foreign team leader: "The only reason we cannot settle this negotiation is because of *you*. You are being uncooperative, you don't listen, you have no business sense. We are going to go to your superiors and we are going to get you fired, once and for all, you stubborn donkey."

He followed this up with: "All the political problems that arise between our two countries [of which there were many] can be laid squarely at your door. It is you, you personally, who are creating very serious trouble, you who are responsible. You are so lacking in understanding, lacking in any sense of responsibility that as far as we are concerned there will be no more meetings until you and your company accept responsibility for all our present problems. Good day."

The Western negotiator was never fired, however, and he continues to be the lead negotiator with the same Japanese to the present day, enjoying a usually amicable relationship with his Japanese counterparts, and philosophically explaining away their threats as akin to those he received from members of opposing football teams in his younger days.

In the Warner–Natsuyama case, the Japanese president reached the end of his tether after many attempts to renegotiate a key clause in a licensing agreement. He too eventually exploded at the Westerners.

In the sugar dispute, the Japanese refusal to accept further sugar shipments was a very daring way of doing the unthinkable, after twelve months of hoping against hope that the Australians would respond sympathetically to their cry for help. In retrospect, it looks like a foolish reaction destined to fail, but in this case the symbolism of refusal was more meaningful to them than rational calculations of success or failure.

There is yet a third example of Japanese "bombshells" that occur during, and especially toward the end of, negotiations conducted overseas. These bombshells often come at a time when the Westerners are convinced that agreement is just around the corner, perhaps even at the moment of signing the agreement. In one instance, a Japanese director, just before putting pen to a major, long-negotiated agreement, suddenly said, "On second thoughts, perhaps we should just check with MITI in Tokyo before we sign, just to be sure there will be no problems on the government's side." And however persuasive the Westerners tried to be, the agreement was not then, nor ever, signed.

The reason anyone "explodes" is, in general, due to frustration. We have, in our own eyes, done our very best, tried valiantly to cooperate, but the other side has not responded, has not listened or been sympathetic. Explosions are often thought of as unpremeditated, but in the cases I've given, and most I know, I have no doubt that they were deliberate, premeditated, and tactical. The authors of the "shylocks," and "get you fired, stubborn donkey" lines had certainly prepared their scripts in advance.

Both these cases are, by any standards, shocking ones. Many Japanese and Western business people who have heard them find them extremely hard to accept. They believe that negotiators who would utter such words have gone beyond the invisible boundaries of permissable commercial behavior. Whether saying the unsayable (or doing the undoable or thinking the unthinkable) is at all cultural among the Japanese, however, is still unclear (but it might be).

In many cases, however, what appear to be cultural differences (in part or whole) on analysis turn out to be rooted in basic human psychology that we all understand. In some of my mixed Japanese–Western negotiation training programs, I use a simple exercise to demonstrate this. I ask trainees to discuss and decide on a set of polar adjectives to describe personality differences that will best distinguish between those present. Usually, they settle on "outgoing versus introverted, shy" or something close to those. I ask all the trainees to rank themselves in a line with outgoing people at one end, introverts at the other, then pair together the more outgoing ones with the more introverted to exchange mutual perceptions of one another and actual experiences with the opposite type.

Two lessons always emerge from this. One is that all of us have a lot to learn about how to get along better with people very different from us (even if we are from the same culture). Examples include, for extroverts, speaking more slowly, allowing more time for answers, not crowding the other person; and, for introverts, speaking up more, being more friendly, being less intimidated.

The second lesson is the "sleeper." The dynamics of an encounter between an outgoing person and an introvert closely parallel those in business encounters between Japanese and Westerners. The complaints of both sides are close to the complaints of extroverts and introverts. At base, then, improvements in the face-to-face skills of international negotiation will often be improvements in our ability to relate to and deal with people whose personalities are extremely different from our own.

Chapter *6*

Japanese Attitudes Toward Contracts

One of the least understood and most exasperating aspects of the Japanese is their attitude to contracts and the law. For instance, the Japanese will conduct million-dollar transactions based on no more than oral agreements. If a snowstorm keeps movie-goers away from the movie theaters, theater owners will ask film companies for a rescission of the movie lease—and get it, with cash gifts to affected theaters, too. A company president threatened with foreclosure uses a sob story to plead for his creditor's sympathy, his wife and children weeping at his side. A Japanese court compels a purchasing firm to comply with an oral commitment to accept delivery of soy beans at the original price despite a drastic fall in the market price. And one of Japan's foremost oil refineries does not demand written contracts merely because its customers dislike such documents of agreement. How does such behavior—irrational and perplexing, if not infuriating, to Western observers*—come about? From what cultural background does it spring?

The fundamental Japanese approach to contracts is to emphasize the relationship being created, instead of the document being drawn up. The traditional attitude toward the written document has been that it is only a tangible acknowledgment of the existence of a relationship between two or more parties rather than a precise instrument that establishes and defines the relationship. Traditionally, and even in many domestic business relationships today, written agreements are not used. The Japanese "mistrust" too much attention being paid to details in a contract. Even when contracts are drafted, their contents are generally vague, with few clauses and only the most important elements of the agreement included. Most Japanese assume that rights and duties under the contract, even when written down, are provisional or tentative rather than absolute. Instead of trying to spell out all possible contingencies and provisions for enforcement in inflexible terms, the Japanese prefer to handle problems as they arise, often recognizing the doctrine of "changed circumstances" (*jijō henkō*). In practice, this has meant that the Japanese have believed that the specific items of a contract are always, even immediately after signing, open to re-negotiation.

In this book, I have quoted a good example of a contract disputes, the Japan–Australia sugar dispute, where the Japanese, in violating the sanctity of contracts upheld by most countries, managed to escalate the conflict into a minor international crisis.

In Japan in 1978, a baseball dispute reflected this same Japanese willingness to break agreements that prove inconvenient. This dispute concerned the attempt of Suguru Egawa, the top collegiate baseball pitcher, to join Japan's glamour team, the Yomiuri Giants. Egawa was drafted in accordance with Japan's baseball league rules to the Hanshin Tigers team, but he refused to join it and signed a contract with the Giants, in violation of the baseball agreement. The Giants speciously insisted that their contract was valid, but, after much dillydallying, the Japanese baseball commissioner eventually ruled that the contract was invalid and that Egawa could only negotiate with the Tigers. The next day, however, the commissioner held a press conference and said that he wanted to see Egawa traded to the Giants before the season began. This led to enormous controversy because the trade of a rookie was prohibited in Japanese baseball. Then the Owners Association came into the act indicating they had no objection to such a trade (prohibited though it was).

February 1, 1979, approached—the deadline for registering players for the new season. If Egawa was not contracted to the Tigers by this date, he would have lost his chance to play in the coming year. On January 31, the Giants announced that Egawa had contracted with the Tigers and that he would be traded to the Giants as soon as his contract was authorized by the league chairman.

The entire league connived in this blatant violation of the rules, bowing to enormous pressure generated on Egawa's behalf by powerful politicians. To save face, punishments of a sort were meted out. The commissioner resigned, taking responsibility for "disturbing people." Both teams punished themselves with self-determined fines. Egawa was suspended from playing for two months. His trade was delayed until the opening day of the season. But Egawa and his backers, in getting what they wanted, showed how fundamentally fragile the rule of formal contracts and agreements can be among some Japanese.

Such cases are representative of the divergence between the typical Western focus on compliance and enforcement and the Japanese emphasis on flexibility and the buyer–seller relationship. I believe that an increasing number of Japanese businessmen are rejecting the older attitudes that disdain the inviolability of the contract, especially in large trading companies and multinationals. I well remember how critical, even scornful, many of my Japanese friends were of the Japanese side during the Japan–Australia sugar dispute, especially of the sugar refiners' rejection of sugar shipments. Similarly, many Japanese were indignant at the Japanese baseball association's conspiracy to break the league agreement in the Egawa case.

However, the fact remains that there are still many Japanese who enter into contracts with non-Japanese assuming that they will be able to vary specific clauses if circumstances change. For instance, one foreign consultant was commissioned to set up, organize, and conduct an international investment seminar for a Japanese company. When, for reasons unconnected with the consultant's efforts, the income from the seminar was not able to cover all expenses (which included the consultant's fee, quoted and accepted in the beginning), the Japanese manager offered only two-thirds of the fee originally contracted. The consultant replied that he had a contract for a fixed fee, but the Japanese manager insisted that it was not a contract, only an agreement, which could be affected by circumstances. Fortunately for the consultant, this view was not shared by a director of the company, who insisted, once notified of the dispute, that the consultant be paid the full fee.

I have had similar experiences myself as a consultant in Japan. For instance, a Japanese consultant and I worked together on a project for a large foreign company. I provided the initial concepts, design, and support, while detail work and final billing was undertaken by my Japanese colleague's company. The agreement was to share profits on a 50:50 basis after expenses had been paid. Problems emerged as a result of differences in the definition of the word "expenses." My colleague arbitrarily deducted, first of all, 20 percent of the fee as his "overhead and tax provision," then his out-of-pocket expenses, such as those of a research assistant, travel, accommodation, and so on, before making the 50:50 split. When I persistently questioned the rationale for the "overhead and tax provision," the Japanese shifted his ground to call it a "tax provision." I then pointed out that since he would not pay tax on expenses or on the dividend to me, the tax provision was excessive and should in any case only apply to *his* portion. It took some time for him to accept or acknowledge the logic. Finally when, through my persistence, he did acknowledge my point, his immediate comment was, *"March-san, kibishii ne"* (Mr. March, you're very hard). I responded that I was only applying the rules of division that he had first proposed, and that "fairness" to both parties was paramount. It was at this point that he revealed what was probably his real thinking from the start.

"But you know, March-san," he said, "business has been very slow for me this year. I have two offices to keep up. I doubt if I can survive." He was now using a standard *naniwabushi* approach.

Faced with what would only, I was convinced, escalate into deeper melodrama, I said immediately, "Well, that is a completely different issue, not connected to our contract." (This was the Western side of my brain talking. The Japanese side knew perfectly well that everything is connected and that logic is inhuman and irrelevant.) "However, I appreciate your difficulty, so I'll reduce my overall figure 10 percent to help ease your situation."

No doubt by some Western standards, I acted foolishly or overgenerously, for I had right and the law squarely on my side. Moreover, by Western standards, he had clearly tried to trick me out of a good part of my entitlement. But in Japan, I feel obliged to be generous, to overlook his, after all, schoolboyish attempt to deceive, for underneath all this is the feeling (at least in Japan) that we are all here on this planet in common cause. This originally Buddhist viewpoint is summed up in a very commonly quoted proverb in Japan, *Sode furi au mo, tashō no en*, meaning "Even the brushing of my sleeve against a stranger's is meant to be" (i.e., is destiny). This man was and is a part of my life, and I could have no grounds for taking a litigious stance toward him. Although in a country other than Japan, I would probably act differently, I hope that the reader can somehow sense what an enormous difference the cultural context makes to one's behavior.

There are two other practical considerations in Japan. First, even if I did decide to sue, it would take years to get to court, and the outcome would be in some doubt. Second, even if I tried to shame him or exert pressure on him in some way in front of business society (i.e., the circle of our common business acquaintances), it would be I, not he, who would suffer, since most Japanese would be shocked at any attempt to use force instead of a mutually conciliatory approach. I learned this the first time I was "deceived" by a client who commissioned, verbally, two business training manuals, which I invested some thousands of dollars in developing. The client, however, kept postponing the training dates for a year, until it became apparent nothing would happen. Angry and perplexed, I luckily had enough sense to ask the advice of Japanese friends. Everyone gave the same advice: "Don't try to use power plays; negotiate amicably with the client." Ample precedents, I was told, involving amicable resolutions of identical problems existed in the world of big companies in Japan. That advice has since served me well in facing many business problems in Japan. Like so many Japanese businessmen, I have learned to be generous when others are in trouble (or claim they are), and to take modest losses to maintain harmony.

LAWYERS

Traditional Japanese reliance on oral agreements and the doctrine of "changed circumstances" to determine claims or to renegotiate, is still widespread and will not disappear overnight. Still, at the core of any business deal or connection is the personal relationship, meaning that the ethical or moral element, rather than the legal, is the central feature of human relationships. This is true even in major trading companies, each of which has a legal department staffed by highly qualified Japanese and often foreign lawyers. As a result of informal inquiries in these companies, I learned that the majority of business managers negotiating with foreign companies do not consult their legal departments—at least, not until the deal has been finalized. No more than 25 percent of business departments consult with their legal departments before that; where there are inquiries, they largely concern foreign law, and in no case have they ever concerned negotiation strategy or any involvement, direct or indirect, by legal staff in the negotiation. While most departments eventually get their legal department to draft the final contract, perhaps one in six business managers even perform that function themselves (the resulting English, say legal staffers, is sometimes a nightmare of unclarity).

With lawyers so infrequently called upon or trusted in Japan, it is no surprise to find how few there are: there are twenty-five times as many lawyers in the United States for each American as in Japan for each Japanese (see the table below).

Comparative Numbers of Lawyers

	LAWYERS		JUDGES		PUBLIC PROSECUTORS	
	Total	Per 100,000 people	Total	Per 100,000 people	Total	Per 100,000 people
Japan	13,200	11	2,800	2	2,100	2
U.S.	655,000	279	27,800	12	23,000	10
U.K.	64,100	114	28,200	50	—	-
W. Germany	47,300	77	17,000	28	3,650	6
France	15,800	29	4,350	8	1,450	3

NOTE: All figures as of April 1986. Figures for judges and public prosecutors in the United States include both federal and state ones. Britain's public prosecution service was set up in 1986.

Source: Ministry of Justice of Japan

Of the 13,200 lawyers in Japan, half are in Tokyo, and only 500 are admitted to practice each year.

It is true that there are large Japanese law offices (although the largest has only 40 lawyers, compared to several hundreds in the United States, and even 150 in Sony Japan) that have impressive international expertise, and whose clients—foreign and Japanese—use them in much the same way they use attorneys overseas. It is also true that these Japanese clients are, for the most part, sophisticated and knowledgeable about Western contractual processes and thinking. However, looking at the broad picture of Japanese business culture, I believe it is true to say that lawyers are not trusted to provide realistic business judgment and tend to be passed over (this is also truer in the West than some might suppose); businessmen trust their own judgments about the other party and the deal; and businessmen in Japan feel secure because the cultural injunction to help a customer in distress is so strong. It is this imperative after all, that underlies the readiness to demand an easing of contractual conditions on the basis of "changed circumstances."

Since July 1987, foreign lawyers have been permitted to practice in Japan, but this is more in an advisory capacity concerning the law of their own countries, not that of Japan. Nonetheless, their entry, bitterly resisted by Japanese lawyers, is bound to have a powerful long-term impact on the practice of law in Japan. One American lawyer has said:

> There is a real danger that Japanese lawyers will be upstaged by the outsiders with respect, at least initially, to business legal matters that involve foreign companies and possibly also those of a domestic nature. The admission of foreign lawyers involves essentially the introduction of the Western approach to the use of rules of law. It is the ultimate step in the integration of business executives and legal professionals in Japan into the world.
>
> With a few significant exceptions, Japanese businesses are not ready to deal with American lawyers with equal professional skill. Many Japanese do not yet have the frame of mind that is necessary for working according to legal rules in the Western sense. They are too wedded to the traditional Japanese approach of achieving mutuality and avoiding confrontation in the course of maintaining business relationships. That negates resort to full negotia-

tion of transactions in advance, which requires careful identification of the subject matter and the reasonably anticipated responsibilities of the parties well into the future. The admission of American lawyers into Japan reflects a major shift with respect to the nature and uses of law. (Freed, 1987)

It can be said, I believe, that the writing is on the wall for the slow demise of the traditional Japanese approach to contracts and the law, if only among the internationally sophisticated Japanese companies. But for the present, it still needs to be emphasized that the contract is not sacrosanct to the Japanese, and Westerners should beware of believing that once they have a contract, any problems will be resolved by its proper interpretation. Except perhaps for such highly complex contracts as financial transactions or construction projects, Westerners would do well to expect continuous re-negotiation and adjustment of contracts with the Japanese.

THE BETAMAX LAWSUIT

Accustomed to the mutuality of compromise in Japan, the first encounter of the Japanese with American legal aggression comes as a great shock. In Japan, when a problem arises, the Japanese will think, first, of conciliation, second, of profusely apologizing, third (if the seller), of correcting any shortcomings in service to the customer. In contrast, the American instinct for litigation seems to the Japanese like the thrashing of a shark when it scents blood. Even Akio Morita, chairman of Sony Corporation, and perhaps the most internationally minded business figure in Japan, was deeply shocked when Sony were challenged, in an American court.

As reported in the *New Yorker*, in September 1976, a letter came to the attention of Sidney Sheinberg, president of Universal Pictures and its parent company, MCA. The letter was from an account executive of the New York advertising firm of

Doyle Dane Bernbach and contained a sketch of a newspaper advertisement that, with Sheinberg's consent, would soon be appearing. "Now you don't have to miss 'Kojak' because you're watching 'Columbo' (or vice versa)," the ad said. It ended with the words "Betamax—It's a Sony."

"Kojak" and "Columbo," two popular television series from Universal, were aired at 9 P.M. Sundays on CBS and NBC, respectively. The name Betamax was not well known to Sheinberg. True, he had in his office a Sony U-matic, a professional videotape recorder that he occasionally used for informal screenings of Universal productions. However, he was soon to realize that the U-matic was only a transitional product in a long effort by Sony to develop a videotape recorder for the home. As Sheinberg mulled over this new product, he began to realize that it posed an enormous challenge to his business. He asked himself if he should let Sony sell this new device, and the answer was: "I'd be crazy to let them." All that MCA's business consists of is selling somebody the right to see—the privilege of seeing—a motion picture or a television program. And this Betamax machine was made and marketed to copy copyrighted material. "It's a copyright violation. It's got to be," he concluded.

A week later, Sheinberg and Lew Wasserman of MCA went to see Akio Morita, the chairman of Sony, and Harvey Schein, the president of Sony's American affiliate, known as Sonam. They met in Morita's New York office, which was on the forty-third floor of 9 West Fifty-Seventh Street, with spectacular views of the Plaza Hotel and Central Park. The meeting started in friendly business fashion with an hour to talk about DiscoVision, the issue at hand, followed by a catered dinner in the Sonam boardroom.

Sheinberg broke the news over dinner. He explained matter-of-factly his company's belief that the manufacture, sale, and use of the Betamax was a copyright violation. Universal would be forced to sue, he said, unless Sony withdrew the product from the market or proposed some other form of accommodation. Harvey Schein recollected that Wasserman added, "We may have to do this because if the Betamax is successful the videodisk (a new product being developed by MCA) will never get off the ground."

Morita told Wasserman and Sheinberg that he found it hard to understand how they could discuss a business deal and threaten a lawsuit at the same time. It was his policy and Japanese tradition, he said, that "when we shake hands we will not hit you with the other hand." Alone with Harvey Schein after the meeting, Morita said he could not believe Universal would sue. "We've done a number of things together over the years," he told Schein, "and we're talking about the videodisk. Friends don't sue." Schein responded that in the United States "you could be the best of friends and sue."

Morita had an open manner and an ebullient self-confidence that made him, to the Japanese way of thinking, an American-style executive. But there were features of American commerce that still troubled him, and one was the American legal system.

By early October, Universal's legal preparations had moved past the memo-writing stage. A private investigator was hired, and he had begun visiting stores that sold Betamax. Without revealing his occupation—but without saying anything strictly untrue—he told sales clerks, "I'm interested in information regarding the Betamax, and I would like to see a demonstration." He was under instructions to observe the copying of Universal productions.

Sony was to be sued on the ground that the act of manufacturing and selling the Betamax and promoting its ability to copy programs off the air made the company responsible for its use.

On November 11, Universal and Disney filed suit against Sony, Sonam, Doyle Dane Bernbach, and several local retailers. Harvey Schein was lunching at NBC when word reached him. He quickly convened a strategy session with several of his subordinates and lawyers. At about six o'clock that evening, Schein put in a call to Morita. "He was getting dressed to play golf—it was Saturday morning in Tokyo," Schein recalls. "I told him that the lawsuit had been filed, and he'let out a kind of death cry. I'm told by people who played golf with him that day that his game was way off."

The trial of *Universal v. Sony* got under way on Tuesday, January 30, 1979, with the opening statements of the two attorneys, and then—kicking off the case for the plaintiffs—a demonstration of the powers of a Betamax. "Rarely has 'The Mickey Mouse Club' had such a high-priced audience of adults," *Daily Variety* reported. "More than a dozen attorneys (probably charging $100 to $200 an hour), a federal judge, and assorted clerk aides watched intently yesterday as a Betamax poured forth the familiar strains of M–i–c–k–e–y M–o–u–s–e." One lawyer squatted on the floor for a better view, and received a lecture from the presiding judge about correct courtroom demeanor.

One witness, Lew Wasserman, had a story to tell. "It has been printed in the Hollywood trade press," Wasserman informed the court, "that when *Gone with the Wind* was put on television there was not a blank video cassette available for sale in the United States. Now, if everyone in the United States ultimately has a copy of *Gone with the Wind*, there would not be much value in *Gone with the Wind* being on television."

Sony lawyers presented their own survey statistics, and documents, and a series of witnesses representing copyright interests with no objection to home taping—among them the baseball, football, hockey, and basketball leagues. A recent speech by Julian B. Goodman, the chairman of NBC, was also quoted. There was no reason, Goodman had predicted, that video recording and broadcast television "cannot grow and prosper alongside of each other." He read from ten years' worth of documents demonstrating an awareness at Universal, MCA, and Disney of Sony's work on home videotape recorders.

"They knew, they did not complain," the Sony lawyer said. "They encouraged. Mr. Morita relied upon their encouragement."

The decision came down in October. "Home-use recording from television is not a copyright infringement," Judge Ferguson wrote, "and...even if it were, the corporate defendants are not liable and an injunction is not appropriate." (The first and subsequent verdicts were appealed all the way up to the U.S. Supreme Court, where Sony, eight years later, won the lawsuit.)

As Schein had put it, "You could be the best of friends and sue." Sony and Morita, and indeed much of corporate Japan, had also learned that unpleasant lesson about the nature of litigation in the United States. Even today, however, there has been no change in the Japanese attitude. Friends don't sue each other in Japan. It represents the ultimate rupture. Any American who would do business with Japan should have these words emblazoned on his shaving mirror.

Part
III

TOWARD BETTER
JAPANESE–WESTERN
NEGOTIATION

Chapter 7

Typical Japanese Negotiation Strategies

In the first chapter of this book, I presented a number of ways—*naniwabushi*, for instance—that the Japanese use to influence the behavior of others. It is time now to look broadly at the whole array of means used by the Japanese in their negotiations with foreigners. Let me now, however, call them strategies and, since there are a number of them, divide them into four categories: normative, rational, assertive, and avoidance.

NORMATIVE STRATEGIES

Normative strategies are ways of behaving that are in accordance with the norms or "rules" of the society. Because they seem so natural, many people may find it distasteful to have them categorized as strategies; the Japanese, in particular, would rather see their everyday ethical behavior as spontaneous and beyond conscious control. Part of the difficulty is semantic, for the word "strategy" has connotations of military offense and calculated behavior that seem disrespectful of the other party. However, I use it here in the sense of a behavior that serves as a means to an end. Thus, all normative behavior—from bowing, shaking hands, appeals to conscience or to high principles—is strategic. It is akin to a set of rules for the "game" of negotiation as played in Japan and for the expectations held of the other side. The violation, distortion, or denial of such rules may be the single biggest source of problems in Japanese–Western negotiations.

Politeness: In all face-to-face dealings with foreigners, the Japanese put the greatest emphasis on behaving properly, being hospitable, courteous, and deferential to those who are senior in age or superior in position, and when they are overseas, they also try to follow the etiquette and customs of the host country. For the most part, this is "insurance" against making mistakes and incurring criticism and being misunderstood, which in itself reflects the abundance of rules in their own society.

Mutual Cooperation and Compromise: Closely linked to this is the view that mutual cooperation and compromise (in Japanese, *gojo gojō*) is a virtue (and much more so than "give-and-take" in the West). The phrase indicates a uniquely Japanese way of solving problems or reaching decisions through a display of goodwill, by mutual trust, and reaching mutually acceptable positions through fine adjustments of one's position or demands. It also relates to the frequent Japanese search for what they have in common with others, Japanese or Westerners, such as common friends, common interests, common goals. This will strike some Westerners as unsophisticated and simplistic, which is exactly what it is. Recognition that most Japanese have simple, unintellectual tastes is a good start to effective relationships with them.

Obligation and Pre-giving: There are a variety of obligations among the Japanese—obligation to society (*gimu*), obligation to one's parents and seniors (*giri*)—but for businessmen the most important is the obligation incurred as a result of favors received (*on*), which should be repaid in some form at some time, although not necessarily promptly or in kind. In Japanese society, obligations to various people are incurred over time, and it goes without saying that a decent man will not forget them and will always be ready to repay them. Obligations and pre-giving also characterize relationships between companies.

Appeals Through Changed Circumstances: Naniwabushi, already explained in detail in Chapter 1, is thought of by many Japanese as *the* Japanese negotiating style. Even the most honorable man in Japan may not be able to honor agreements if his circumstances change for the worst. From the Western viewpoint, Japanese appeals for "help" in the face of changed circumstances are unsettling and hard to refute. In some cases, arguments on such grounds can look specious and raise Western suspicions that the Japanese are prone to panic without analyzing the situation or assessing their options. The Japanese appeal to the Australians to lower the price of contracted sugar seems to be an example of this.

A thorough discussion of what to do when circumstances change, and what guidelines to adopt, preferably set out in a formal contract, may be the best counterstrategy for Westerners to adopt. Note, however, that this is a highly volatile subject to many Japanese, and even to discuss it will require considerable sensitivity to avoid giving offense. At the same time, this type of counterstrategy will considerably reduce the consultation necessary on post-agreement problems, and may foster a feeling of powerlessness that might eventually lead to resentment.

Rightness and Priorities: Michael Blaker (1977) has pointed to Japanese feelings of the rightness and priority of their own goals in prewar diplomatic negotiations. This may be less obvious in business negotiations, but the same feelings do surface at times, serving strategically to maintain team cohesion and to rally public support. This sense of rightness is supported by the widespread conviction that the Japanese are, as a race, decent, honorable, and innocent people. In short, the Japanese sincerely believe that their society is a moral one and they a moral people. Words or actions that imply otherwise are the shortest route to ending a relationship.

Persistence: Morsbach (1980) has demonstrated that persistence is one of the great Japanese virtues in negotiation, while Blaker (1977) has pointed to the constant reiteration of the same offer, with little or no variation, as a central feature of Japanese international negotiation style even in the postwar era. Persistence comes to the fore when negotiating positions have resulted from a consensus, since even in business the Japanese often try to avoid any concessions that tamper with their original positions. This is the key difference from "give-and-take" negotiation, where reciprocal concessions need not be disturbing.

Buyers Outrank Sellers: The Japanese prefer to wait for the other party to make the first offer, especially if that party has come to them. This proposal then becomes the starting point for their own deliberations. This is partly because buyers always outrank sellers in the Japanese business world. Among the Japanese, this difference in status is clearly marked by the deferential behavior of the seller, who uses honorific language, and, conversely, by the mildly haughty manner of the buyer. Japanese buyers often express skepticism about sellers' propositions, whether they be Japanese or foreign, due to a fear that their claims for their products are inflated. At the same time, the expression of skepticism serves as a conscious tactic for generating useful product knowledge and market information to guide the final decision. Perhaps this is not too different from the situation in other countries, although many foreigners tend to find Japanese buyers less friendly and more aggressively direct. The obvious moral is for businessmen to go into meetings with Japanese buyers thoroughly prepared to answer all questions about market prospects, competition, product manufacture, and performance.

RATIONAL STRATEGIES

Rational strategies are those pursued to achieve economic or pragmatic results, or to promote greater efficiency in communicating and negotiating.

Team Organization: It is generally true that Japanese organize their teams more quickly than Westerners, and that they are consistently more cohesive throughout negotiation. In many cases, the Japanese team will have worked together before and have developed fluent teamwork and confidence in its own abilities as a team. This is the most formidable and professional team one can face. Sometimes, however, the team members will be meeting for the first time, possibly because an ad hoc group of people has been brought together from different departments for this particular purpose. The first meetings of these ad hoc groups can seem painfully slow to Western eyes, as members have to feel one another out. Who knows what, and who is likely to be a suitable leader? Sometimes even two meetings are needed just to crystallize views about who will take the initiative in a negotiation. By and large, Japanese refrain from taking any initiative in a poorly structured setting, and so everyone sits around seemingly determined not to do anything. By contrast, even at a first meeting, members of Western negotiation teams will have no hesitation about putting forward ideas on how to win the negotiation or what strategies to use.

The principal concern of a Japanese team is to clarify its own position. That clarification only comes about when something resembling a total consensus on the company's requirements emerges. If different departments, factions, or interests persist in raising objections, there will be no decision until those objections are resolved. (Only rarely will top executives step in when committees become bogged down on important projects.)

By Western standards, this necessity to develop a consensus can exact a serious toll, for it means that the negotiation may begin without the Japanese team having a consensus, in which case they will probably temporize and shilly-shally. Again, it can mean that their pre-negotiation discussions have not covered alternative strategies or contingency action plans. So much energy has been devoted to clarifying the team's position and developing a consensus that the more rational, Westernized, business-school approach of "which of a number of strategies is best" does not emerge. This may result in the Japanese side coming into the negotiation totally unprepared for anything else except one proposal. Probing questions on other issues may not be answered, and such apparent lack of thought may make the Japanese appear ill-prepared, evasive, or both.

A typical example of this was a Japanese government negotiation to set up an institute in conjunction with a foreign country. A memorandum of understanding had already been drawn up, and the two teams met to handle implementation. Japanese preparation consisted mainly of specific proposals about funding, staffing, housing, with some brief internal discussion about types of projects. The Western team, however, put its initial emphasis on conceptual issues. What should be the overall philosophy of the institute? By what principle would costs be apportioned? What guidelines should be used to decide on projects? When negotiations began, the Japanese immediately presented their concrete plans, budget statements, and timetable, but the Westerners brushed these aside. First, they insisted on discussing the philosophy and concepts, but the Japanese were clearly not taking this in. To the Westerners, the Japanese reactions looked like tactical blocking or puzzling obtuseness. They started to speak tartly to the Japanese, making the Japanese retreat further into silence and ambiguity, which served to intensify Western irritation.

Such cases are not uncommon. Frequent Japanese failure to respond to Western conceptual discussion is best understood as due to the pragmatic focus of the Japanese on things to be done, or as a result of narrow instructions to the team concerning solely practical issues. An extended postponement may be needed for the Japanese to prepare for discussions of conceptual questions.

One team of researchers on Japanese negotiation style has written that "the Japanese bargainers will. . . bring with them a carefully considered agenda" (Graham and Sano, 1984). I suspect they have in mind Japanese representatives of major companies who arrive in the United States with a well-prepared set of proposals that have been thoroughly debated and then approved by the board of directors. However, when the Japanese team is factional in character, with representatives from different departments or different companies each with competing interests, or when the negotiation is a re-negotiation under changing market conditions, or when the Japanese have little international experience, preparation to negotiate concretely on all the issues may be limited or incomplete when the negotiation begins.

Building Trust: The building of mutual understanding and trust is the key element of initial contacts in Japan. The Japanese often open first meetings with lengthy speeches on the company's history and achievements, expressions of goodwill and hopes for the future, followed by rapport-building, informal chat, such as "Is this your first trip to Japan?" or "How was the trip?" and friendly discussion of family matters, common interests, knowledge of each other's country, sister-city relations, and comments (always positive) on hospitality received. Through such conversation, the Japanese show how important it is to them not to be strangers but to have various mutual interests that will enable both sides to work together harmoniously.

The Use of Amae: Japanese businessmen strive to move toward a family-type relationship with their partners, whether foreign or Japanese. In Japan, an important aspect of such relationships is the degree to which "dependency" (*amae*) can be developed. *Amae* has no exact English translation, but it concerns dependency on the goodwill of others. In everyday life, it is used most commonly about a child's pleading for some special favor from its mother. In adult life, it embraces any personalized attempt to receive special favors over and above what is customary or contracted. If there is really a familylike intimacy between the two parties, reciprocity can be expected.

In many case studies in this book *amae* is an important, underlying dynamic that is usually reciprocated but sometimes frustrated. *Naniwabushi* is grounded on *amae*. Hathaway's frustrations as a commodity account manager resulted from the skillful way his clients built the relationship to a level of intimacy where *amae*-based pleas were hard to refuse. Saviola of Nippon Texacom especially offended the Japanese telephone company official because he left no room for the exercise of an *amae*-based plea. The Australian sugar negotiators rejected the Japanese *amae* pleas for special help.

Information Orientation: The Japanese are information-hungry. They ask many questions. Some questions are part of the trust and dependency building stage, some are straight attempts at character assessment, while some may contribute to their assessment of the situation at hand, for example, "How do you view the current market situation?" Even in informal junior-level meetings, there are always questions about business. Any information gleaned, irrespective of how it is valued by the recipient, is likely to be reported in writing.

This information-orientation is formidable and needs to be

recognized. I was involved in a negotiation many years ago where there was a serious leak of confidential information on my side. A junior member of our side had had dinner with two junior Japanese members, who asked him with great subtlety about the attitude of our team leader toward some key proposals. To questions such as, "I suppose Mr. A is strongly opposed to the idea of..." the young American innocently replied, "Oh no, he's in favor of it." In this way, they were able to obtain a very clear picture of our position. Since that time, I have always emphasized the need for caution in informal discussions, and the importance of Westerners reporting all discussions in detail, since even the questions themselves may reveal what the other side considers important.

Padded Offers: Do the Japanese pad their opening offers? Do they make a practice of beginning with an outrageous bid? Looking across the board of my own experience, the answer is clearly no. In fact, one of the commonest Japanese complaints against Americans is that the latter are insincere and not to be trusted when they make an outrageous offer. This suspicion is strengthened if the Americans, soon after making such an offer and comprehensively justifying it, shamelessly change it to one closer to reality.

In Japan, beginning with an outrageous bid is called "the banana-sale approach" (*banana no tataki uri*), which though rare in Japan seems to be used on occasion by Japanese when they are overseas. Graham and Sano (1984) state that this happens when the Japanese "don't know what to expect from foreign buyers and they feel that it's safer to leave room to maneuver."

The Use of Middlemen: As Graham and Sano (1984) point out, "business relationships in Japan are established only through the proper connections and associated introductions." Cold contacts, without a proper introduction and out of the blue, are not effective with the Japanese. Someone reputable should introduce you, speak on your behalf, say who you are, emphasize your advantages and interests. This middleman may be a bank, a trading company, a buyer, or a supplier to the target company, but until you can find the appropriate person to introduce you, it is wiser to make no approach.

Middlemen are also used during negotiations to provide hard-to-acquire information about the other side, or to help resolve problems and conflicts. Unlike Western negotiation teams, it is rare for the Japanese decision-maker to be present in the team unless a decision is imminent. If persistent problems arise with the middle managers in the Japanese team, a Western decision-maker will be impatient to bypass them and talk to their top man. The appropriate way to accomplish this is through a middleman rather than through direct contact. This may lead to an informal meeting between the top men on each side, but precisely how far the Westerner should go in that meeting depends upon his assessment of how eager the Japanese are to conclude a deal. The less eager they are, the more indirect and general should be the statements concerning the problems. At the same time, the idea of using a middleman may merely block a creative search for solutions to the problems. The Warner–Natsuyama case demonstrates that creative strategies are still the key to handling negotiation problems. It is worthwhile to keep the middleman as a last resort for defining the problem rather than as a direct means to a solution.

Concealing the Top Man: This negotiation strategy of the Japanese is fascinating in the way it reflects their rank-consciousness (Kawaguchi, 1986). It is a kind of role-playing within the team done in order to affect the impression given to the other side. When talks become complicated and intense in the bargaining stage, younger members in the team are put forward to talk to the other side about all the troublesome details that are unpleasant for the senior Japanese to mention. The higher-ranking remain uninvolved until the time is right for them to reappear and introduce some "power" to settle the problem. Even when the Japanese team decides to yield on a specific issue, the final approval is given only by the top man, with the younger members still looking unhappy about the concession. This is a conscious strategy because the team will decide beforehand on the "actors" to play certain roles: the "bad guys" who bring up all the difficult issues and the "good guys" who show the generosity to concede. These roles and actors cannot be reversed, for if the older members—who hold more power and are the decision-makers—were to act stubbornly on small matters, it would give a mean impression of the company. When younger members behave in such a way, the other side can interpret it as lack of experience or mere youthful impatience.

Through this tactic, the Japanese team tries to increase trust in the company as a whole, thus making the negotiation smoother. Moreover, because of the hierarchical structure of Japanese society and its consciousness of status, the obligation to reciprocate is stronger when a person with a higher status yields rather than when a junior member does so.

The Use of Concessions: In Japan it is customary for the seller to give the buyer a discount or a premium (called *"sabisu,"* or "service," in Japanese) when agreement is reached. When I signed a contract to have a realtor handle the sale of my Tokyo condominium, the sales manager made me a present of a battery-operated shaver and a telephone card, total value about ¥3,000 ($20). When I renewed the insurance on my car, I was given a set of towels, valued about ¥800 ($3.70). Even if you don't ask for a discount on, say, furniture, a smaller store might give it to you anyway when you agree to buy.

The same attitude prevails for bigger deals. If the Japanese side want to reach an agreement, and your remaining objection is not unreasonable, they may not only concede on it but also add something else to demonstrate friendship and sincerity. This could take the form of covering some expense your side had incurred or would incur in the future.

Behind-the-Scenes Activity: The Japanese show a fine delicacy in raising issues at informal discussions that might prove embarrassing in formal meetings. Requests for price reductions, discussion of new items, notification of news (personnel changes, new business activities), or expressions of emotion can be easily handled informally. I advise Westerners to use this means to the full and to appoint their most personable man to handle such communications.

ASSERTIVE STRATEGIES

Assertion and aggression are not pronounced features of the Japanese national image, but rather indirectness, patience, and perseverance (along the lines of Suzuki of the Toyosan case). However, the cases we have studied show that there is more than image to the Japanese.

Bulldozing: What Blaker called "push, push, push" is part of a pattern of persistent and aggressive determination to achieve one's ends, come what may. Yamashita in the Warner–Natsuyama case, or the sugar refiners once they had decided to reject all further sugar shipments, or Nippon Steel in its long history of high-handed dealings with Australian coal and iron ore sellers provide concrete examples.

What makes the Japanese such remorseless "bulldozers"? The fear of loss of face, the conviction that they and their position are correct, and a masculine aggression focused on winning are all factors. However, I believe that pushing and bulldozing "skills" are declining among the Japanese, for the toughest Japanese in these cases were all raised in prewar years and comprise a type that may be disappearing.

Lecturing from High Moral Grounds: In Japan's hierarchical society, leadership is the responsibility of seniors, even among teenagers. In the *"sempai–kohai"* (elder–younger) relationship, seniors have the responsibility to guide, instruct, counsel, and correct the behavior of juniors. Guidance, for the most part, is given through subtle hints to make the recipient aware of the problem without it being pointed out specifically. When people are not perceptive enough to recognize such indirect hints, and do not obey promptly or perform efficiently, they can expect at least a tongue-lashing from their senior (as many company presidents receive from their mentor chairman).

No such danger exists in negotiation with ordinarily gentle Japanese businessmen. Nonetheless, Japan is still a hard, rigorous society for its members, and most people, when carrying out their senior, responsible role, have had occasion to speak severely, critically, accusingly, and indignantly as they preempted some high moral ground. If a Japanese wishes to discipline a junior, a lecturing approach is the only effective cultural model available. This is especially so if the "junior" is of another culture. Heart-to-heart talks may be ruled out by language deficiencies, lack of time, and the tactical loss of advantage by coming down to the other's level.

Tactical Questioning: Graham and Sano (1984) point out that the Japanese ask many questions because in their decision-making process everyone must be convinced. There are, however, other reasons for such questioning. First, it can be a device to maintain a sense of control, of having the upper hand. Many Japanese are particularly skillful at this. Second, questions can be used to see if your team's proposal holds up under close scrutiny. In this case, questions posed by you in return may be ignored. Third, questions can be used to buy time or to conceal a lack of knowledge.

Tactical questioning is not widespread among the Japanese, but if a Westerner is faced with questions being repeated, the following approach (modified from ideas presented by Graham and Sano) could be used: 1. Summarize your previous answer after such statements as the following: "I already gave that information to Suzuki-san yesterday, but to reiterate..." or "That's the same question we talked about before, but I'll go over it again"; 2. Offer to write down the requested information so that it may be shared with all concerned executives; 3. Generally, a repeated question should be answered the second time in about ten minutes. The third time it's asked, the answer should be a one-minute summary. If the same question is asked a fourth time, there are two possibilities. The Japanese are wanting specific information from you but are not getting it, and they do not have sufficient language skills to ask the right question. In this case, you can say: "We feel that we've already answered this question before, but perhaps there is some other information you are seeking that we haven't given you yet. If so, would you like to rephrase your questions?" Or it may be a persuasive tactic and not for gathering information. The appropriate response then may be silence or a change of subject.

AVOIDANCE STRATEGIES

Of all the strategies used by the Japanese, whether in international negotiation or everyday life, avoidance strategies are the most diverse, the most subtle, and the most culturally comfortable. Much of the Japanese approach may be summed up in the proverb of the three wise monkeys who see no evil, hear no evil, and speak no evil. It is positively virtuous to be like a wise monkey in Japan, particularly when it spares someone who has said or done something improper or offensive.

The Use of Silence: "Silence is golden," "The mouth is the root of all trouble," are just two of the many Japanese proverbs that praise the virtues of silence. Silence also keeps you out of trouble, for everyone seems wiser when they keep their own counsel. Open your mouth, and who knows what criticisms you will draw.

The respect for silence in Japan also extends to response time for answering a question. In the West, if you don't answer promptly, you will be thought rude or cunning, but not so in Japan. Even answers that are clearly not answers will be accepted. When asked a difficult question, a Japanese businessman may reply "That's a good question. Let me get back to you on that," when in fact the question has floored him. Or he may simply shake his head and smile wanly, suggesting that the question is completely beyond him, or he hasn't really understood it, or it should have been asked by someone else.

Wait and See: In many cases the Japanese do not like to take the initiative or "reveal their hand," so the primary negotiation tactic of the team may be to "wait and see" for as long as possible. Deferrals and postponements are aspects of this tactic.

If something disagreeable has happened, the Japanese opposite number may just not be available—as happened to Hathaway. Other related tactics include withholding friendship that has previously been given, appearing hesitant, and claiming no decisions have been made. At least some of this can be thought of as pure perversity, a refusal to behave in the way the other side expects, grounded in resentments against a particular foreigner or foreigners. The perverse communicator should be distinguished from the nonassertive communicator, who really wants to avoid someone or feels threatened and shows his feelings through a defensive or retreating body posture.

NONVERBAL EXPRESSION

Strategies for concealing, for avoiding communication, for "becoming invisible" are called avoidance strategies, and they are as native to negotiation as the poker face is to playing poker. The Japanese, exceptionally skillful at nondisclosure, at masking and restraint of emotions, are indeed hard people to read, especially for the inexperienced Westerner. Are they master deceivers or supreme tacticians, you may ask. Neither of these apply, I believe. Nondisclosure is deeply ingrained in Japanese culture, and the remainder of this chapter is devoted to demonstrating how the Japanese communicate nonverbally.

Learning to put a "face" over one's true feelings and emotions is part of growing up for every Japanese. He or she learns that the direct expression of emotions, especially through the face, is uncultured and even improper. Rather than express feelings without reserve, a Japanese filters his or her feelings so that when they are expressed, it is in a form that is neither offensive nor esthetically unrepresentative. This process can be aptly described as "dressing up one's true feelings for public consumption," a dressing up that extends not merely to the words employed but to all other nonverbal means of communication, such as facial expression, clothes, body language and stance, gestures and hand movements.

True feelings must be refined through the innumerable rules of social behavior and social roles that lie at the heart of Japanese society. The rules specify what can and cannot be said, and even the manner in which something is said. Is the occasion appropriate for a woman to play winsome girl, pragmatic housewife, or warm mother? Is this the right time for a man to be deferential, or is gutsy macho more appropriate? Should he, on this occasion, ensure that the feelings of the other party are protected, even to the extent of total fabrication?

Behavior that is finally decided on as permissible, fit for public consumption, in all its verbal and nonverbal dimensions, is called *tatemae* in Japanese. The word means something like "official policy," and the nuance is very close to the English phrase "dressed for public consumption." This is the antithesis of *honne*, "one's true feelings and thoughts." Thus, *tatemae* is equivalent to "face," not indeed a fixed face, but the face that is suited to a particular occasion, with all the nicely articulated— one might say crafted—modalities of nonverbal expression.

The deeply ingrained habit of behaving in a *tatemae* way is critical to the Japanese ideal of social harmony and to the realities of maintaining harmony among people who are raised to pursue, first and foremost, social acceptance.

In Japan's *tatemae* society, the appearance, or front, or face of the individual is like a blank sheet upon which he can write whatever expression the occasion calls for. In repose, you see this in the apparent Japanese impassivity, an impassivity that is not unvalued, for it serves to mask the emotions, to rest and daydream behind, or to avoid something undesirable in his surroundings. While Japanese impassivity provides a cover for many moods or purposes, what is perhaps most typical of the Japanese is that it covers, not deviousness or Machiavellian cunning, but passivity—in the sense of being submissive, lacking forcefulness, inert. Many Japanese are natural followers, waiting for direction or guidance, unresisting and submissive to their superiors or intimates. With strangers they are different— they avoid strangers, avoid contact even of the eyes, masking themselves behind impassive faces and conservative clothes and unobtrusive behavior. The Japanese who face you across the negotiating table will often be like this.

Using psychological concepts popular in the West, the Japanese "face" in the broadest sense masks a people who are insecure and in search of identity and acceptance. In their constrained, largely immobile society, most Japanese can never escape the lifelong web of dependency relationships—with mentors, superiors, parents, older brothers and sisters—and rarely achieve adultlike independence or real friendships in the Western sense. The interpersonal relationships or identity they achieve are, for the most part, determined by their jobs or social roles. These are all on the *tatemae* level, often attained at the expense of denying their true feelings, of day-to-day living in the smooth but painful dishonesty of *tatemae*. In other words, Japanese society tends to make people depend on others for psychological satisfaction, values, and identities. Japanese nonverbal behavior is easiest to understand, and accept, when this cultural background is recognized.

Technically speaking, there are many varieties of nonverbal communication, and one that is well-documented is the language of gestures. In Japan, pointing to the nose is a reference to oneself, scratching the ear signifies perplexity, raising the thumb means someone is being referred to, usually a boss or husband, and so on. Gestures like these, with their standardized meanings, are a fabricated language, and so say nothing about the existential man, about you and your feelings at any given time.

Another fascinating mode of nonverbal expression is clothing and its associated elements of make-up, hairstyle, and accessories. As I have already indicated, the Japanese preference for conservative attire and neatness in both men and women reflects a strong trait of social prudence or behavior free of risk. This same motivation to play safe and stay with the pack also underlies Japanese readiness to pick up and then drop fashions and other fads. In fashion-conscious (meaning conscious of what others are doing as well as wearing) Japan, it is risky *not* to be fashionable.

I will here concentrate on the ways in which the Japanese express their feelings and emotions nonverbally. This is no easy task, however. If we were studying animal behavior, it would be easy to point out standardized behavioral patterns used to express emotions. But human beings, unlike animals, can choose their behavior and expressive patterns, so it is not easy for anyone to read the real meaning of nonverbal behavior. In what follows, I will report my own observations on the Japanese use of some of the most important "communication equipment"—the eyes, mouth, and hands, and body posture and movement.

The Face: Japanese culture demands that its members maintain an immobile, impassive social face in most situations, an exercise in control that takes years of training to achieve. Japanese children are like kids everywhere: playful and naturally expressive. By adulthood, however, the cultural lessons have been well learned, and the most common facial expression is the *"shirankao,"* literally, "knowing nothing face," a blank, uncomprehending exterior. *"Shirankao"* is used by the Japanese when the individual wishes to avoid communication or involvement. For instance, a Japanese with a hangover may pass an old friend in the street displaying a *shirankao* and give no greeting. Among the Japanese, this would be accepted tolerantly, but foreigners who socialize with Japanese find the practice upsetting.

However useful *shirankao* may be in making everyday life smoother, there is a price to be paid. If you spend your whole life learning how to suppress your natural feelings, you lose the ability to portray feelings through the spontaneous patterning of facial muscles. You end up being a one- or two-face man. Hence many Japanese adults, apart from being able to smile with modesty and show surprise, find it almost impossible to portray other facial emotions.

The other most-utilized face among the Japanese is to express surprise, which is a form of flattery. The expression is the same as with Westerners, but it is often exaggerated, sometimes to a melodramatic extent. The eyes widen, the forehead is elevated, the mouth opens, and the countenance expresses an admiring wonderment at the speaker's conversation. The surprise look may be accompanied by a long-drawn-out *"ha-a-y-y-y,"* which is formed at the back of the throat with the mouth open and the tongue flat. This expression of surprise is replete with pleasant implications: that the speaker is erudite and the topic is absorbing. Surprise functions as a major means of appreciating others in Japan and is highly valued as courteous behavior.

Besides the blank look and surprised expression, the Japanese face usually says little more. The eyes and the mouth are the two places to watch. If someone, Japanese or not, is angry, the eyes will usually narrow and the mouth be pursed in a thin line even before the individual himself becomes conscious of his feelings and starts to process and suppress his emotions. When the Japanese regains control of himself, he is likely to adopt a *tatemae* face, so the time for reading what is going on is short and demands a supersensitivity to nonverbal behavioral changes.

The Eyes: Traditionally, it was considered disrespectful and dangerous to look into another person's eyes, especially those of a senior. Even today, a majority of the Japanese avoid embarrassing eye contact with others, and find relief in prolonged "necktie" contact with foreigners.

The Japanese close their eyes frequently, often in situations where it would be regarded as discourteous by other races. When listening to a lecture, it is commonplace for the Japanese to close their eyes or look down and never to look at the speaker. During business meetings, when space is more confined, many Japanese sit with a passive body stance and their eyes closed, often for the entire meeting. A Western speaker in a meeting relies on eye contact to gain feedback on the impact or understanding he is achieving, as well as to optimize the effect of nonverbal flourishes and emphases he may add to the presentation or lecture. To the Japanese, different customs of using the eyes prevail.

For instance, some Japanese will keep their eyes partially closed—somewhat in the way eyes are supposed to be in Zen meditation—when only about 60 percent of the eye is open. This lends a sleepy, withdrawn, mildly scared look to the face. Even if the Japanese are listening with their eyes fully open, they may not focus on the speaker but on something in the middle ground, but with an air of not really concentrating on anything at all. In either of these cases, my experience has often been that the individual is listening carefully. The Japanese often indicate their degree of receptivity to another's speech by other physical cues, notably frequent nodding, an open body stance, or an inclination of the body toward the speaker.

There is a convention among the Japanese, largely tacit, that if you do not or cannot see something, it does not exist. This turns out to be a useful rule in crowded cities like Tokyo, whether on the pavement or on the road. If you are walking on a crowded pavement, you can, as a Japanese, play the *shirankao* game: walk with head down, look at your feet, or read a newspaper, whereby you make it the other man's responsibility to avoid you. The point of this game, which is also played out on the highway, especially when lanes of traffic are merging, is to avoid eye contact. If you are in the weaker position, as when you are violating a give-way rule or breaking into a queue, making eye contact loses you your advantage.

As a foreigner traveling in Japan, you may therefore see a great deal of seemingly odd behavior, such as two people sitting side by side and apparently talking not to one another but to themselves, since they always look straight ahead, never at each other, and do not even incline their bodies toward each other. But that conclusion would be almost certainly incorrect, for even if there is no direct eye contact, the Japanese is well aware of what is going on. His specialty is peripheral vision, looking out of the corner of the eyes at what is interesting.

On occasions when Japanese wish to express aggression, it is the eyes that are likely to be used. For example, where you are the violator and you make eye contact with a Japanese who is angry at you, he is likely to use his eyes to fix you with a steely hostile gaze to communicate his feelings. The mouth will be drawn in a tight line, the shoulders squared off, and the body immobile to focus attention on the eyes. I noticed my barber do this with his daydreaming assistant the other day. Without uttering a word, he turned toward the boy and fixed him with a hostile stare to have him remove the apron from me and sweep away the hair. Among the Japanese, there is no ambiguity in such communication, and the guilty party is much more likely to respond with an apology, without the verbal repartee that enriches such clashes in some Western countries.

The Mouth: The Japanese are prone to compose their mouths neatly, closing them firmly but relaxedly, with greater awareness put into the upper lip so that it protrudes very slightly when the face is in repose. Opening the mouth is something to be avoided in Japanese etiquette even today. This is consistent with the general cultural injunction against expressiveness, and it is abetted by the paucity of labial consonants in Japanese, which permits the Japanese language to be spoken quite easily with the mouth virtually closed.

However, the Japanese do use the mouth expressively for some purposes. To express their difficulty or uncertainty about a matter, they may form the mouth into a neat "O," perhaps inclining the head slightly to one side and pushing the lips forward. Women often cover their mouths with their hands to hide sudden immoderate laughter or giggling. At times of bewilderment or uncertainty, the hand might instead be put on the head, or women may pull at a lock of hair, or place two fingers, the index and middle fingers, across the mouth. The meaning of all this hand-on-mouth, mouth-pursing, and related behavior has intrigued me for some time. My interpretation is that the Japanese, when surprised or caught off guard, automatically reach up to their face to check that "the mask" is still intact. Indeed, much preening—and the Japanese do a lot of it, such as checking the line of a coat, removing fluff from clothing, checking one's hair—is all to check the "mask," motivated by the many anxieties of a *tatemae* society.

The Hands: Every Japanese learns to use his hands and fingers in supple and competent ways. There is a rich repertoire of children's games emphasizing manual dexterity—string games, jacks, games requiring the hands and fingers to be moved at high speed—as well as early instruction in the use of scissors and knives. Hand gestures are common, and young female pop singers usually have hand and arm movements coordinated with their songs that become their "signatures" and are imitated by millions of children. The Japanese are proud of their manual dexterity: handicrafts are widely practiced, and precision, neatness, and sureness in handling delicate things and in wrapping objects is commonplace.

However, hands are poor instruments when it comes to expressing feelings and emotions, unless used in conjunction with other parts of the body. At the most, hands are used for rapid or random movements or to express a person's discomfort or some aspects of his personality.

The Japanese tend to fold their hands away. Shaking hands is alien to most Japanese, and it is comical to see a man rub his hand briskly against his trousers (to clean the hands) before he shakes hands. In traditional dress, neither the arms nor the hands feature in the line of the costume, the hands are often tucked within the kimono or the full sleeve. Standing formally, waiting in line at an official function or making a speech, convention dictates that the hands be clasped together in front of the body. This softens the body outline and lends a deliberate submissiveness to the posture.

Hands become expressive when they alone are performing an action. In a short story by the famous writer Ryunosuke Akutagawa, a mother hears of the death of her son with a faint smile on her face. To the observer, she seems serene until he notices that she is almost tearing a handkerchief she is holding in her hands to shreds. The author comments, "She was crying with her two trembling hands." This story illustrates a more general principle of Japanese nonverbal expression. Due to a general physical impassivity, an emotion may be indicated merely by restricted activity in one bodily region.

Movement and Posture: Japanese and Westerners differ quite fundamentally in posture. Japanese posture is maintained by balance and control coming almost entirely from the buttocks and upper thigh muscles, with the weight distributed down through the leg and balanced on the foot in front of the heel (in contrast, Westerners balance more on the ball of the foot). The arms do little to maintain balance among the Japanese, a fact that is probably reinforced by the need to rise effortlessly from the *tatami* mat floor without pushing up with the hands. In the tea ceremony, a celebrant balancing a tray of delicate utensils, rises from the *tatami* through balance achieved by leg, buttock, and stomach muscles. The same independence of the upper body from the tasks of maintaining bodily balance are seen in most martial arts, in Noh drama, in traditional Japanese dance, as well as in everyday life. It makes for a more flat-footed stance and better bodily balance, which you can note in Japanese pedestrians waiting to cross the road. They tend to "sit" deeper in their lower bodies, balanced on both feet. It also makes for shorter steps and for more awareness as the foot is placed on the ground at each step.

These distinctive features of posture and movement become important in understanding the feelings represented by certain nonverbal behavior. For instance, in situations of fear or awkwardness, where a Westerner might walk away or stand up assertively on the balls of his feet, the Japanese are likely to retreat into their buttock-centered lower body balance. This both looks and is defensive, a kind of rootedness to one's territory.

There is quite a remarkable cultural difference related to this. When faced by some imminent threat, Westerners are prone to face it defiantly, moving their body weight forward. In contrast, the Japanese tend to settle down into their lower body, turn their back on the threat, and squat down in a tight ball or put their arms over their heads. This avoidance and nonseeing response occurs throughout everyday life in Japan (for instance, in reaction to earthquakes or lightning at home, attackers on the streets) and has close analogies in Japanese responses to international threats.

Group Synchrony: The cultural emphasis on intimacy and getting along well with others is reflected in the ways the Japanese tend to synchronize their movements with others. Most commonly observed is the frequent nodding that occurs during a discussion. This is called *"aizuchi"* in Japanese, which originally meant the alternate hammering by blacksmiths on the anvil. *Aizuchi* is also a courtesy, indicating that one is listening closely to what is being said and that the words are agreeable. *Aizuchi* is thus a major means of achieving synchrony between people as they move through a conversation, nodding to each other and echoing one another's words.

When a group of two or more Japanese is moving together, they achieve synchrony by adjusting their pace, length of stride, and body angle, to the other members of the group. This synchrony seems to be based on the same passivity, or a greater willingness to surrender to intimates, as I noted earlier. Indeed, without surrendering one's independent will, there cannot be effective synchrony. Thus, for instance, when two lovers are walking together, they synchronize their body movements perfectly. It can also be detected when friends of the same sex walk together. Synchrony is even seen when one group member stops, or looks bewildered or surprised. Unselfconscious mimicry by the others is almost instantaneous, serving as a means of deepening intimacy through the sharing of common experiences. Note that this mimicry and sharing is essentially nonverbal; if a foreigner were able to suspend his intellectual evaluations and simply follow the group flow of movement, he would, I am sure, have no difficulties in experiencing intimacy with a Japanese group. This would be at a nonverbal level where the Japanese are most unaffectedly themselves, where they are least hidden behind the *tatemae* mask.

Westerners have long remarked on Oriental and, especially, Japanese inscrutability, and many feel ill at ease when confronted by it. In the process of affirming that such inscrutability exists, I am also suggesting that behind the impassive face there is very little real threat. Submissive waiting, mild avoidance, and use of the appropriate social role to decide on a suitable face are common. Deviousness, craft, calculation, or sinister design are uncommon, but if there is a strong emotion, it is unlikely to remain concealed for long.

Chapter 8

The Japanese Negotiator:
An Assessment

Earlier I quoted the viewpoint of Dewey of Neuerbach Japan
that North Americans are "somewhat naive in negotiation"
compared to the Japanese. Hathaway, the commodities dealer,
and even Midway, the metals negotiator, would probably
agree. Yet there are also many cases of Japanese negotiating
naively; the cases of the sugar dispute and the broadcasting
companies could be cited. Moreover, as I have already mentioned, the Japanese have little opportunity to develop their
bargaining skills in everyday life. Can the view of them as "better" negotiators, then, really be supported?

JAPANESE STRENGTHS

In my observations of many Japanese negotiation teams, from
pre-negotiation to caucus-period discussions, they have ranged
from highly experienced to inexperienced. In spite of this wide
difference, I detect certain characteristics that reflect how the
culture itself predisposes even naive and inexperienced Japanese businessmen to negotiate in a secure, parsimonious, and
cautious manner.

Teamwork: As a rule, the Japanese always form cohesive

teams, even if composed of strangers. These teams may not always be well led or well managed, but they do have clear leaders whose leadership is respected, in contrast to Western teams where everyone wants to be a negotiator and leadership often becomes nominal and cohesion minimal. Japanese team membership is also more flexible in that fresh players can be readily substituted.

Position: Developing a unified team position and then getting consensus, i.e., the support of the whole team for the position adopted, generates even greater team cohesion and support for the leader.

Bargaining: Once a firm position is achieved, the Japanese strongly commit themselves to it and give little thought to bargaining or making concessions to achieve their goals. Most Japanese negotiators I have spoken to, however, do say that they are usually prepared to give modest concessions, perhaps 10 percent or so, but they tend to feel offended if a Westerner asks for 30–40 percent concessions, because this means the foreigner is assuming that the Japanese have made an initial offer far different from what they are really prepared to accept.

Lack of Hurry: The lack of a sense of deadlines or pressure of time makes the Japanese supremely calm.

In looking at how American and other Western businessmen manage negotiations, there is no doubt that they are often vulnerable on each of these points and are easily intimidated by apparent Japanese solidarity. In contrast to the Japanese, their teamwork is poor and their position fragile, not considered or secured. Thus they easily make concessions in the mere hope of reciprocity, thus damaging their own position. Finally, they can be in such a hurry that they make concessions merely to meet some arbitrary deadline.

In Japan, Western negotiators quickly learn from the Japanese to make these four factors a basic part of their negotiation style. They learn to function as a team, with one spokesman only. They learn to establish a position that all agree on, and not to change it except in a private team meeting. They also learn to be patient and to look for nonmonetary offers and other inducements they can make rather than just chipping away at the price.

True, such adaptation can mean changing elements of one's own natural style of doing business, but that is merely a sensible cultural adjustment advisable anywhere. Moreover, it leads to more effective deals and relationships with the Japanese.

JAPANESE WEAKNESSES

Communication Skills: Many people, including the Japanese, have spoken critically of the Japanese as communicators. In my first days in Japan, I was most impressed by the sociability of the Japanese, especially their skills in making visitors feel welcome by solicitous inquiries about their views and situation. Like many Westerners, however, I came to find a good deal of coldness and distance after the initial period. This was puzzling to me, and I have only recently come to make sense of my experiences. The Japanese people are generally good at interpersonal communication that deals with information exchange, and the exchange of news, views, opinions, gossip, and experiences in a friendly, relaxed way. They are, moreover, polite and well mannered, and it is important to remember that "manners" are themselves a form of communication. On a scale of human communication that culminates in true intimacy and openness, however, communications that are concerned only with manners or information exchange are of a somewhat limited nature. To achieve genuinely open and intimate human relationships, more is needed—friendliness, interest in the other party, perceptive insight into his or her heart and mind (for often an individual is unable to clearly express what is in his or her mind, and it may take an outsider's insight to achieve that), and thus true understanding. Regrettably, many Japanese have serious limitations in their ability to achieve such an understanding with people they are not familiar with, that is, strangers or foreigners. Too often, they project themselves as cold, unfriendly, disinterested, and seem to lack the skills necessary to understand others in a human way.

In negotiations, the Japanese can sometimes be singularly unobservant because they tend not to look at the other side to pick up nonverbal clues, and because (when English is the language of negotiation) they are preoccupied by the tasks of translating and retranslating rather than with the flow of the conversation. Poor communication skills, in turn, stem from their lack of intimate contacts or friendships. They have underdeveloped skills at making friends on their own initiative, and may sometimes be intimidated by, or even jealous of, Western skills in this area. It is usually better to be restrained in the early stages of negotiation with the Japanese until you see what sort of man you are facing.

As discussed elsewhere, many Japanese tend to be like the lead negotiator in the case of the broadcasting organizations, placing their emphasis on intuitive understanding, and so being quiet and receptive during negotiations. Although many Japanese feel they have strong intuitive powers, my personal experience suggests this is not true when they deal with non-Japanese. My advice, in any case, is to take great pains in spelling out your message so as to minimize misunderstandings, along the lines recommended to Warner Foods in the Warner–Natsuyama case.

Consensus Can Be a Dead Weight: As discussed at various points, agreements once made by consensus are often exceedingly difficult to revise, even if there are compelling reasons. Even when the Japanese position proves to be untenable or inferior, most Japanese leaders will persist at trying to get your agreement to their position rather than summoning up the courage to re-negotiate within their own organization.

Easily Offended: Yamashita of Natsuyama was unquestionably offended by the behavior of Warner's Murray. The bureaucrat that Texacom's Saviola had to deal with was quick to take offense at an unintended slight on the whole Japanese race. Prudence about your jokes, reflections upon Japan as a whole or upon individual Japanese, is most desirable.

At the same time, many Japanese are easily intimidated, as the psychiatrist Okonogi has pointed out (see page 26). This is also connected to feelings of awkwardness or inferiority many Japanese experience when dealing with Westerners. Such factors easily weaken their ability to perceive clearly or deal evenhandedly with problems.

THE HUMAN DIMENSION

The Japanese people have a deserved, if stereotyped, reputation as being modest, hardworking, quiet, and polite. By some standards, you might think that they would be "push-overs" in negotiation. But they are not. How can we make sense of this? Let me try to do that by emphasizing that individual Japanese learn a great deal of role flexibility in their culture: they learn to switch social roles readily. Applying this to "typical" Japanese negotiating behavior, we can say that there are two dimensions of behavior—politeness versus arrogance, businesslike versus ambiguous, plus the peculiarly Japanese trait of melodramatic emotionalism—that make most Japanese negotiating behavior easier to understand. These are part of the well-established, cultural way of behavior in Japan, and most Japanese businessmen would feel capable of behaving in any of these ways because, depending on the situation (that is, according to whether one is superior or inferior, whether there is urgency or otherwise), they are expected behaviors that others will go along with.

Below I give in tabular form, some of the behavior that may be expected in different stages of a negotiation.

Seven Typical Negotiation Behaviors

NEGOTIATION STATE OR SITUATION	LIKELY STYLE OF THE JAPANESE
Opening meeting	Polite, bland, friendly
First business meeting	Polite, businesslike, a little cool
Japanese team has difficulties coordinating, reaching consensus	Polite, ambiguous
Foreign side has internal problems—weak, obstructive or uncooperative	Directive, businesslike
Foreign side rude, offensive, causing loss of face	Disdainful/exclusive withdrawal (arrogant ambiguity)
Foreign side aggressive, seems to have upper hand	Ambiguous, bland, noncommittal
Agreement is close, desired	Polite, ready to be accommodating

This shows that, depending on the situation, the same Japanese negotiator can present faces as diverse as poker-faced detachment, quiet attentiveness, friendly encouragement, remorseless attack, or bulldozing arrogance. Not every Japanese, it is true, can do all these, but the situation, and his role in it, may be more important than the man himself in bringing out the culturally appropriate behavior.

If you recognize that most Japanese have this kind of (admittedly limited and standardized) role flexibility when they serve as their company's representative in a negotiation team, you can probably feel able to accept that the polite, bland, friendly

Japanese face that initially confronts you is only the tip of an iceberg. In short, you will not underestimate him or dismiss him as lightweight merely by first impressions. Because self-concealment and self-disparagement are so thoroughly practiced by the Japanese, no Japanese cares to judge another by first impressions (unless they are obviously offensive first impressions).

Studying the cases in this book, we have been able to see how each side perceived the problems and how they were finally resolved, sometimes according to the strategies and intentions of the actors, but at other times fortuitously. In the process, the Japanese characters who appear in the cases are shown to be diverse—open-minded, narrow-minded, nervously introvert, refreshingly extrovert, cold and tactical, generous and deeply human, smooth communicators, chronic avoiders, amusing, humorless. At the everyday level of characterization, then, there is little room for facile stereotypes about the Japanese national character. On the other hand, I am convinced that some generalization is possible and desirable when we speak specifically about and focus on commercial negotiation behavior. There are, as I pointed out at the beginning of this chapter, striking similarities in the ways that different teams of Japanese prepare for negotiation, in how they manage the process, and how they react to the unexpected. Moreover, whether it is team or individual negotiation, the Japanese, as we see repeatedly, are more organizationally constrained than most non-Japanese by the imperatives of their consensus decision-making style, by the politics of their in-house factions, by their customary caution and skepticism, and by the absence of the key decision-maker from the front-line negotiation team.

All of this means that Japanese organizational behavior, especially a person's behavior in a group and the behavior of the group itself, is heavily standardized, heavily regulated by rules and guidelines that pervade the whole society. Individual Japanese, even at a senior level, have little or no freedom to behave other than as expected; in particular, they have virtually no freedom to vary offerings already agreed by consensus. What this means to a practicing negotiator is that the best chance for him to sway Japanese thinking is right at the beginning, using a comprehensive opening statement (as recommended in Chapter 9). It means, I believe, that Western negotiators have to be much better prepared and to have thought out all their options thoroughly before the first meetings. If you show that you have done your homework and that your position and approach are reasonable and well-founded, the Japanese will listen. If you only bring up your ideas in a piecemeal way as the negotiation proceeds, it may then be too late to influence their thinking. Remember, if you are in Japan, that the team facing you is only part of the group you have to bring around to your way of thinking.

Finally, don't be the victim of your assumptions or stereotypes, or of mine either. There are, for instance, exceptions to every generalization I have made in this book. Don't assume that the Japanese facing you is either a traditionalist or a Western-minded person, or that he has no power to vary proposals or make on-the-spot concessions. Ultimately, when on a certain day at a certain hour you face a certain Japanese in a certain frame of mind, you will be on your own. Be prepared for that occasion. Discover and study the diversity of the Japanese as negotiators. Learn from the mistakes that others have made.

Chapter 9

Improving Japanese–Western Negotiation

The purpose of this final chapter is to develop ways in which Japanese–Western negotiations can be managed more effectively by first identifying the problems that arise and then developing counterstrategies. This is not as simple as it might sound, since negotiation is not a single activity but a multifaceted process, a chain of stages, each with its own character, needs, and demands. The various stages, including postponement, caucus or review, and conflict resolution, for purposes of discussion will be narrowed down to five stages: 1. The pre-negotiation stage, the preparation before we first formally meet with the other side; 2. The opening stage, the first formal meeting or that part of it concerned with greetings, social conversation, and exchange of general views or perspectives; 3. The bargaining stage, when each side makes its demands clear and attempts to elicit or offer concessions; 4. The complication stage, when relationships become, at least momentarily, "sour" or off-balance, and irritation or aggression are expressed verbally or nonverbally.

When it comes to detailed analysis of what problems occur at each stage of a Japanese–Western negotiation, I am able to supplement the cases in this book with forty-five realistic role plays that I have designed, conducted, and analyzed since 1980 featuring teams of Japanese businessmen pitted against teams of Western (usually American) businessmen. Participants in these programs had an average age of thirty-seven, and most of them already had some international experience. To undertake a role play, two teams of four to five people are formed from each national group, and each team receives its own "brief," consisting of negotiation instructions that are at variance with the other team's and that usually produce mild conflict between the two sides before an agreement, if any, is reached. These role plays are highly realistic and involving, and the technique enables us to focus on the mistakes made by individuals and teams, and to find out by post-negotiation analysis why each side did what it did. Each team gives frank feedback, and the upshot is to provide a rich simulated experience.

THE PRE-NEGOTIATION STAGE

There is no doubt in my mind that inadequate preparation prior to the start of negotiation is the single biggest problem in negotiation, domestic or international, Japanese or Western. Preparation, however, involves a large number of diverse factors, from team development, formulation of objectives and strategy, analysis of the situation, definition of problems, evaluation of the environment and of the other side, to development of an agenda, procedures, and arrangements, and game plan development. W. F. Morrison (1985) has written a useful book entirely on the subject of negotiation preparation, indicating how substantial a subject it is.

Culturally, there are sharp differences in the way Japanese and Westerners prepare for negotiation. The Japanese priorities are, first, to develop a working organization around a discussion leader, who will usually become the spokesman; second, to ensure that everyone has a thorough understanding of the issues; and, third, to develop a position on which everyone can agree. This position is usually arrived at in what we might call an intuitive way, for there is rarely any discussion of position options. The essence of the Japanese approach is organization, and they can be expected to come into a negotiation with a cohesive team, a single spokesman, a shared understanding of the issues, and consensus on one position even if they are ill-prepared in other respects.

In contrast, Americans and Europeans make the following their priorities: first, to understand the issues; second, to debate possible strategies and positions they could adopt and reach some majority agreement on initial and second-line positions; and, third, to try to assess the likely approach of the other side. So the Western approach is predominantly strategic, with little or no attention paid to team leadership, cohesion, or to achieving a genuine consensus on position.

The serious consequences of such lopsided preparation in face-to-face negotiation cannot be stressed too strongly; for Westerners discover that they are less committed to their position than the Japanese, and are readier to make concessions in order to reach agreement. Westerners, irritated by the rock-solid commitment of the Japanese, may attempt to persuade them by vigorous argumentation, directed not only at their spokesman but at other team members, although I have to say that I have never seen this approach succeed. It has only resulted, ironically, in worsening the internal cohesion and commitment to its position of the Western team, for failure to influence the Japanese leads to internal dissent over new strategies.

Another aspect of preparation that needs thought by Westerners is in their selection of a suitable team leader as spokesman and negotiator. Westerners have a curious ambivalence here. A great deal has been written in the West about the ideal qualities of a negotiator. Karrass, Graham and Sano, Kniveton and Towers, and many others have developed lists of the characteristics desirable in a negotiator. Kniveton and Towers are perhaps representative when they specify "unlimited patience," "persuasion," "knows himself as others know him," "knows and understands others," "good socializer," "strongly committed but can be flexible." This emphasis reflects interest in individual negotiators (not team performance), and it is true that Westerners can be capable individual negotiators. On the other hand, there is a good chance that a team of Westerners will be inferior to either one competent Westerner operating alone or to a cohesive Japanese team.

In contrast, the Japanese behave as though they do not believe that the spokesman of a negotiation team has to be an outstanding or even especially competent negotiator. To them it is sufficient if he follows instructions, is supported by effective teamwork, and has in his team people who do possess good negotiation skills (though they may not be suitable as spokesmen). This approach is based on the more fundamental, if intuitive, view that negotiation management is a multidimensional skill. Thus many skills are needed for effectiveness, and since few individuals have that diversity of strengths, a team is to be preferred. In fact, since the Japanese frequently change their team members, such as by bringing in juniors when awkward issues have to be dealt with, or more senior people when the talks are close to agreement, they also demonstrate a recognition that different situations require different skills and fresh approaches, somewhat like substitution in basketball.

THE OPENING STAGE

With their penchant for establishing sound human relations, the Japanese place greater emphasis upon trust-building social conversation at the beginning of a negotiation than do Westerners. This pre-business small talk, handled in a friendly and sympathetic way, typically covers travel, quality of accommodation, mutual friends, and sports (especially golf). Five or ten minutes spent in this way establishes an amicable relationship with most Japanese groups.

Internationally inexperienced Westerners dealing with the Japanese usually avoid personal conversation and dive head-first into business discussion. One transcript of a Japan–U.S. negotiation shows the Americans getting down to business as soon as introductions are finished. A Japanese begins with a personal question, but it is brushed aside.

Japanese: Have you visited Tokyo?
American: We really haven't had any time yet to see anything. I thought we'd open with the letter of the twenty-third.

Thereafter it is all business until suddenly this snatch of conversation emerges:

American: Do you mind if I smoke?
Japanese: OK.
American: By the way [claps hands], I'm Ed. This is Walter.
Walter: Hi.
American: We might as well call each other by first names.
Interpreter: It won't be easy to call you by your first names. This is not a Japanese custom. Please call us by our last names.
American: Is there a reason for that? It's not an easy thing to always do that. (McCreary, 1986, pp. 78–79)

The Americans here are both ill-at-ease and culturally unsophisticated, and would be seen so by their Japanese opposite numbers. Although this particular negotiation. reportedly ended with a mutually rewarding agreement, sending cultural unsophisticates to represent your organization is not recommended, since their chances of giving offense will increase as the negotiation proceeds.

Another common problem in the opening stage is to assume (as Americans often do) that a negotiation is nothing but a set of specific items or issues, each to be settled independently. This is not the way the Japanese see matters. Whereas Americans are prone to proceed point by point, from the beginning of the first meeting, many Japanese (at home, if not abroad) will often begin with the general issue, talking unsystematically around it, meandering without agenda or structure, and thoroughly annoying their counterparts with a seeming lack of logic or of a plan. This conversational meander, in fact, is a part of the process of becoming comfortable with one another, of building bridges, and is common in many Asian countries. Those who would deal effectively with the Japanese should learn to go with the flow of conversation in this opening stage, confident that the time will soon come when you can both get down to business with an agenda mutually agreed on.

In many international negotiations, when the actors may have little or no prior experience, they will be unsure how to proceed. As a result, they may fail in the opening stage to check that both sides share the same understanding of what the negotiation is about, what special terms or expressions mean, what has been agreed up to that time, and, not least, they omit to communicate to each other their interpretation or slant on the subject (which will be the basis of their attempt to persuade the other side to their way of thinking). The failure to do such things creates a variety of problems later, from misunderstandings to distorted perceptions, which can eventually lead to hostility, postponement, or abandonment.

THE BARGAINING STAGE

This stage begins when one side makes concrete proposals for acceptance by the other side. The broadest difference in this stage is the Japanese desire to achieve an overall agreement first (for example, in a joint venture negotiation, to agree only on capitalization, a broad mission statement, and a manning profile), versus the Western desire to negotiate point by point (for example, in a similar joint venture negotiation, Westerners typically want to hammer out policy for each area, especially marketing, personnel, R & D, and product development, whereas the Japanese would want to leave these to be settled after the agreement is concluded), with the final result being overall agreement. However, if the negotiation is for a simple deal, such as a commodities purchase where only price, delivery, and quality have to be settled, the bargaining style of Japanese with substantial international experience (which you can check by discreet questioning) will usually be similar to that of Westerners.

This bargaining stage also sees Westerners much readier to make concessions than the Japanese. Westerners tend to use what they believe will be persuasive, "winning" arguments, but these rarely achieve their goal. The Japanese tend to be skeptical of such arguments, and may analyze them semantically, search for hidden meanings, insist on them being repeated, or apparently ignore or be unresponsive to them to such an extent that the Westerner may become impatient, lose the thread of his own rhetoric, and readily make concessions in order to speed up and complete the negotiation process.

In contrast, the Japanese bargaining style is slower, more deliberate, with much time given to re-stating and re-clarifying their position to the other side. It takes a comparatively long time for them to make concessions, and this only happens when they feel they are close to agreement in other respects.

THE COMPLICATION STAGE

The problems that emerge from these contrasting negotiation styles and stem, in turn, from the values of two very dissimilar cultures, can color the entire negotiation. As persuasive and strategically creative as Western teams can be, the Japanese can be psychologically better prepared for complex negotiations. Their patience, indifference to pressures of time, and cautious style repeatedly show up as more rooted and stable than the more volatile Western style. Their team structure, organized usually around one spokesman, is important, for he is the one who puts requests, makes demands, or offers concessions, and then only after he has checked with his team or his boss. Most likely, as the negotiation unfolds, most Western members will speak up spontaneously, even interrupting one another, on occasions making sudden new offers or changes in proposals without checking with the rest of the team or the spokesman.

Western negotiators often have great confidence in their persuasive oral abilities, but unfortunately the Japanese are not very susceptible to Western-style persuasion, which is likely to leave them skeptical and occasionally even suspicious of debatelike persuasive statements. So, when Japanese negotiators register no reaction to a Westerner who has forcefully argued an iron-clad case, we can anticipate a quick build-up of disbelief and possibly annoyance in many Westerners. The likelihood of a direct confrontation then increases, and it is but a step (as I have seen more than once) to name-calling, petty animosity, or hostile eye-balling (on either side). The list below presents some reactions that occur when complications emerge.

Japanese
1. Are less concerned with pressure of deadlines;
2. Retreat into vague statements or silence;
3. equire frequent referrals to superiors or head office;
4. Appear to slow down as complications develop;
5. Quickly feel threatened or victimized by aggressive tactics or a stressful situation.

Western
1. Are more conscious of time/feel pressure of deadlines;
2. Become aggressive and/or express frustration sooner;
3. Often have more authority for on-the-spot decisions;
4. Fail to understand, or else misinterpret, Japanese nonverbal behavior;
5. The breakdown of team organization, with members competing to out-argue the Japanese and control their team.

RESOLVING INTERNATIONAL NEGOTIATION PROBLEMS

The above analysis indicates that problems can arise at every stage of cross-cultural negotiations. What can be done about resolving these? If we had to take each of the problem items listed above and work on them in turn we would probably become so lost in detail that no improvement could be made. On the other hand, if we look broadly over the shortcomings, we can achieve both a new comprehension of what the international negotiation process is, and of the kinds of strengths, skills, and practices needed to be successful at every stage of negotiation.

Five Necessary Skills for Effective International Negotiation: In reviewing the cases and other data cited here, at least the five following key skills seem to be needed to manage the negotiation process fully.

1. A high level of interpersonal communication skill on the part of the negotiation team leader and spokesman.
2. The ability to analyze situations and develop a comprehensive understanding of complex matters.
3. The ability to think clearly and act strategically without offending the other side.
4. Effective teamwork throughout the negotiation, so there is always adequate preparation and planning.
5. Continuing awareness of and reflection on the ongoing negotiation experience, so that team members are constantly aware of what is happening in human as well as strategic or business terms.

In Japan, there is much discussion about the importance of businessmen becoming more international in outlook. Until recently, however, this concept of an "international man" has been used in an ill-defined way, with few attempts to state precisely what such a man is or in what way he can be developed.

Recent research (Ratiu, 1983 and March 1984) has demonstrated that a genuine international type of man does exist and has shown that such a man is an effective communicator who watches and listens carefully to others; deals with situations pragmatically; does *not* think that he has special skills (such as patience, flexibility, broadmindedness, empathy); is highly aware of himself, his feelings, thoughts, and especially stereotypes about people from other cultures; and checks his own tendency to stereotype foreigners against his observations of the foreigners he is dealing with.

In contrast, less international managers operate not at the level of actual experience but in terms of theories or categories formulated before they meet with the individuals. They talk about the specific skills that are needed to adapt to foreigners; they compare people of different nationalities as though there were some objective standards that made this possible; they compare, evaluate, and search for explanations of differences, rather than looking closely at the actual experiences they are having. These managers usually end up confirming their own stereotypes, whereas the truly international man tends to modify his stereotypes as a result of experience.

Understanding the concept of an "international man" helps to make clear that negotiations involving controversial or sensitive matters are likely to be most successful when the negotiators are people who do not use pre-judgments or stereotypes to reach conclusions about other people. As we have seen, some Japanese–Western negotiations end in frustration or conflict because the negotiators fall back on negative stereotypes of the other side, which leads to blaming and name-calling, rather than dealing with every issue in its own right and defining problems with a view to solving them.

The following table by Ratiu (1983) provides a fuller picture of the differences between managers.

Differences in Approach Between the "Most International" and the Other Manager

	Other Managers: an objective macrostrategy	"Most International" Managers: a subjective microstrategy
Goal	Adaptation to society, to the macroculture	Adaptation to individual people, to the microculture
Requirements	Special skills required for adaptation, such as patience, flexibility, broadmindedness, empathy, honesty, etc.	No special skills required; instead, adaptation is seen as dependent on the pragmatics of the situation
Assumptions	Objectivity: stable aspects of the world are objective, externally recognizable facts	Subjectivity: stable aspects of the world are subjective, internally recognizable impressions
Process of adapting to a new culture	Experience	Experience
Question	Why is this happening? Search for explanations and reasons	What is happening? Search for descriptions, interpretations, and meaning
Relevant data	Facts are the relevant information, external information known about country from past experience or present situation	Feelings and impressions are relevant, as well as internal personal reactions from previous similar situations and present situation

	Other Managers: an objective macrostrategy	"Most International" Managers: a subjective microstrategy
Process	Comparison and evaluation: attempt to differentiate new culture quantitatively from known culture(s)	Description: attempt to differentiate cultures qualitatively without comparing them
Result: internal	Confirmation of stereotypes, theories, and models	Modification of stereotypes, clarification of impressions, pictures, and interpretations
Result: behavioral	Socially withdrawn, intellectualizing, judgmental	Socially engaged, flexible, open

THE FOUR STAGES OF THE STRATEGIC NEGOTIATION PROCESS

An area as full of challenges and subtleties as negotiating with the Japanese has long invited many people to search for practical guidelines to action more effective than relying on intuition or "common sense," and less unrealistic than striving for total insight into the Japanese. My own guidelines or approach, growing out of a long period of consulting, training, and research, I call the Strategic Negotiation Process (SNP), and since 1984 I have included training on the use of this SNP in all the international negotiation courses I have conducted in Japan and the Pacific area. Its most important elements are team development, opening the negotiation with a comprehensive statement, delayed bargaining, and a quick resolution of conflicts.

Team Development: Western teams are often assembled in a cavalier, thoughtless way, which is reflected in their performance. Probably the worst negotiation teams are headed by in-effective leaders or spokesmen, where the team members are not comfortable with each other or supportive of the leader, where the members have similar perspectives or skills and so lack breadth of outlook or intellectual diversity, where there is no prearranged agreement on who will speak, who will manage, who will be nonverbal observers, who will coordinate intra-team communications, and so on.

Much more time needs to be spent on team development by Westerners. This means developing genuine teamwork and spirit, and support for the leader, who, of course, must be the right person in terms of authority and prestige—but these alone are not enough. He also needs, for instance, to be an able com-municator with people who are not native English-speakers. Team members, too, need to be intellectually as well as ex-perientially diverse, analytic, intuitive, quick, people who are creative strategists, effective communicators, attractive social-izers, capable presenters, as well as being basically sound negotiators themselves. At some point in a protracted negotia-tion, such people will be much appreciated. Once the team is picked and its members understand their mission and roles, a trial negotiation against a group who simulate the other side may greatly strengthen confidence and preparation.

Opening with a Comprehensive Statement: There was a time when, as a young negotiator, I took pride in my ability to "wing it," to enter a negotiation with minimal planning, confi-dent I could win out using my "wits" alone. I no longer think this way, for I have learned in Japan how important planning is in achieving the kind of long-term agreement I want. On the basis of my own and others' experience, I now recognize that an opening business statement, comprehensively and per-suasively presented, is critical to serious discussion of the topic and to the quality of the agreement you achieve. This statement should say how your team envisages the background, the key issues, and current trends in the environment or marketplace, especially those that have led you to adopt your general stance toward the issue under negotiation.

This opening statement provides the best and perhaps the only opportunity to present the full scope of your views and approach (thereafter, discussion invariably shifts to details). The statement should be well planned, well researched, and well structured, deliberately designed to persuade the other side that one has sound, well-supported reasons for taking any subsequent positions. However, it is not recommended that you offer such a concrete offer or demand until all conceivable issues have been presented and your side has developed comprehensive understanding of the other side. The benefits of the extended opening statement are: first, it is a practical countermeasure to minimize the development of conflict arising from premature bargaining; second, it puts emphasis on substantive issues, not positions, and keeps it there; third, the Japanese are culturally accustomed to, and appreciate, such an approach, and will listen carefully, as they did in the Warner–Natsuyama case.

Delayed Bargaining: As I wrote earlier, Western negotiating teams are more likely to begin bargaining prematurely. As a general rule, offers or demands should not be made until you have learned as much as you are able of the other side, "where it is coming from," what its real needs and interests are. Unreasonable or excessive demands usually originate either from a psychology of panic or fear—panic that something bad (from some other source) will happen unless you cooperate with or assist them, or fear that you will take advantage of them unless they take the initiative and put you on the defensive. We can learn from the Japanese how to handle these situations, namely by not reacting, not showing annoyance, and not making an immediate counteroffer. Instead, it is better to try to learn, by asking questions, where the other side's motivations are: is it fear, bluff, or what? Even if the offer you are made by a seller is, to your surprise, well below what you were prepared to pay, one should neither show that surprise, nor accept the offer, for it may be that you have, in fact, badly miscalculated the prevailing market price.

The buyer who offers an extraordinarily low price—and the Japanese often do this when overseas—is probably hedging against being caught. What he needs is to be reassured that the price you are prepared to sell at is a reasonable one. The onus is on you to produce such reassuring data. But if he is merely bluffing, what should you do? Personally, if I were convinced that the other party was bluffing, I would simply decide not to do business with him, for I have tried to make it a rule in Asia (and elsewhere) only to do business with someone I feel personally comfortable with, and whom I can trust. I've never wanted to trust bluffers, and that would also be true of the vast majority of Japanese.

Asking for more information, rather than getting enticed into a bargaining exchange, delays bargaining and allows you to be better prepared. Whether Westerners can benefit from this advice no doubt depends on their ability to be more indifferent to time in negotiations. Coming to Japan with a fixed departure date and a subsequent packed schedule is the worst possible basis for effective negotiation with the Japanese.

Quick Resolution of Conflicts: Irritation, annoyance, hostility, resentment, conflict—all these are quite likely to emerge during sensitive negotiations with the Japanese. The Warner–Natsuyama case is the best example of a conflict-ridden negotiation that I know, and the process by which conflict was resolved is similar to the formal one presented in the table given below. In the first stage, the Warner people were acutely aware of their own feelings of conflict and frustration. In the second stage, after they unsuccessfully tried to understand what the real issues were, they turned to an adviser, a Japan specialist, who

How to Handle Conflicts in International Negotiations:
A Four-Stage Approach for Effective Conflict Resolution

As soon as you become aware of conflict or frustration in the negotiation, apply a conflict resolution approach, as follows:

FIRST STAGE: RECOGNIZE THE TRIGGERS OF CONFLICT / FRUSTRATION, SUCH AS: *You and/or other side:* Feel threatened Feel defensive Are lectured to, spoken down to Stop communicating	*SECOND STAGE:* i) ASK YOURSELF: What is the *real* issue here? Clarify your own feelings, thoughts, needs, objectives once more. ii) ASK OTHER SIDE FOR: Clarification of any misunderstandings. iii) BE INSIGHTFUL: How does it feel to be them? Ask again: What is the *real* problem?
THIRD STAGE: HONESTLY RE-STATE POSITION For improved mutual understanding	*FOURTH STAGE:* DECIDE YOUR STRATEGY TO RESOLVE CONFLICT E.g., recess, informal talks, apologies, cooling-off period Discuss real issues, accept responsibilities

was able to provide them with understanding and insight into Natsuyama's behavior. The third stage saw the Warner president make an honest reappraisal of Warner's position and the history of the relationship, which led to his formal presentation to Natsuyama (fourth stage), when he discussed the real issues (one of which was his own style) and accepted responsibility for the problems that had occurred.

However, the Warner–Natsuyama conflict took several months to resolve, when the ideal is to resolve difficulties as soon as they arise. To defuse conflict, the most common strategy is to recess and to caucus, which is effective with the Japanese. Another effective move is simply to apologize or express regret, which the Japanese are also quick to do. Where possible, informal talks between the two leaders alone may also be valuable.

USING THE KEY SKILLS

If you have built an effective negotiation team, you should have included people especially strong in such skills as analytic ability, communication, insight, strategy, and persuasiveness. Strength in these areas will enable a team to deal with all the problems that may arise at each stage of negotiation. The following table shows the skills specific to each negotiation stage. While this has an academic flavor to it, there is an important lesson here. Most negotiation team spokesmen, like most people, are only strong in a limited number of areas. They may be good leaders, but poor strategists or persuaders. Conversely, in their team they may have people of exceptional insight or persuasiveness who, however, would not quite measure up as leaders or spokesmen. Therefore, people should be used and consulted with, in the areas of their strengths, both human and business. This principle is an important part of the technique for effective negotiation team leadership.

We can now look at each of these five skills in more detail.

Key Skills at Each Stage

NEGOTIATION STAGES	SKILLS				
	ANALYTIC ABILITY	COMMUNI-CATION	INSIGHT	STRATEGY	PERSUA-SIVE NEGOTIA-TION
PRE-NEGOTIATION	●	●			
OPENING MOVES	●	●	●	●	
BARGAINING				●	●
COMPLICATION	●	●	●	●	
AGREEMENT					●

Analytic Ability: This is of major importance to the pre-negotiation stage, which includes the analysis of the situation, modeling, mapping, predicting, and estimating functions, as well as clarifying the content of the agenda, location, conditions, and procedures of the negotiation. This is similar to the Japanese *nemawashi* process of preparation, but also includes consideration of the external environment, analysis and understanding of the other side and its situation, preliminary definition of terms, as well as organization of the team and its leader, which are less stressed by the Japanese.

Informal contacts between the teams are necessary to gain agreement on location, procedure, agenda, and so on. These contacts also provide an excellent opportunity for each side to inform the other on the specifics of their national negotiation style, for example, how senior the team members are, their decision-making practices and powers, involvement of background figures (stakeholders, such as banks, government departments, industry associations), which is particularly desirable for Japanese teams in view of cultural differences. Oral or written explanations, and, better still, sound or film slide presentations can be effective in educating the other side and minimizing misunderstandings. Naturally, a general rule in international negotiations is to make as few assumptions as possible about what the other side thinks, how it functions, what particular words mean when used, or the "real" meaning of words or actions.

Communication: You can think of international negotiation as an abstract or conceptual exercise, but the fact is that two sets of people—with their own emotions, allegiances, expectations, interests, sensitivities, objectives, and cultural backgrounds—deal with each other in a totally real situation. Therefore the processes of human communication—expressing oneself clearly and unequivocally, listening and being listened to, being empathic, asking for and receiving feedback, being sensitive to and respectful of each other's feelings—have to be incorporated into the cross-cultural setting. First establishing a working relationship on a human level is more important than presenting inflexible positions or pressing for demands or concessions.

As regards facilitating communication and solving problems, three of the biggest problems are inaccurate perceptions, strong emotions, and misunderstanding. Here are some ideas on how to handle these:

1. Inaccurate Perceptions: Put yourself in the other person's shoes. Try to understand how he sees the world. Try to get past the positions he presents, to his underlying needs and interests (e.g., Is he under pressure from his organization? Is appearing to win important to his prestige, perhaps after a series of "failures"?)

2. Strong Emotions: Allow others to be emotional and to "let off steam." This often has the effect of defusing tension, pro-

vided that you are prepared to be generous and not hold it against the person. The Japanese, raised in a culture that values self-control and the concealment of emotions, often consider strong emotions to be undignified and ugly. But they will not hesitate to be emotional when they feel it is the only way to teach others a lesson. Non-Japanese need to be wary about copying this, since there is a special danger that the Japanese will feel they are the aggrieved, injured party when someone attacks them "unfairly." Of course, if this happens, it is highly irrational, but not something to be debated at that point.
3. Misunderstandings: Avoid misunderstandings by using the most basic and important of human communication skills. First listen actively. Keep checking that you understand. Ask questions, give feedback by means of facial expression, seek restatement of any difficult point ("Could you say that again in a different way, please?"). Second, acknowledge others. When you speak, ensure that you are understood by defining your key terms, repeating these points, summarizing, inviting questions, and asking questions that can test the other party's understanding.

When you ask questions, always wait for the answer (Japanese usually take longer to answer because they are translating backwards and forwards in their minds). Never assume that your question was misunderstood, or ask another question without getting an answer to the first. To do so is profoundly confusing to everyone. However, you can assume that your question may not be clear.

Never forget that English is not the native tongue of the Japanese, however fluent they sound. The most prudent step is to use interpretation throughout formal meetings.

If you find that you personally have persistent problems in any of these three areas, perhaps someone else should be your team's spokesperson. It is no discredit to have problems in this role (almost everyone does), and you may make your best contribution as a team member.

Insight: As the negotiation proceeds, both sides need to be properly prepared and knowledgeable about the other. Knowledge is needed about the interests, real needs, internal politics, external affiliations, and so on, of the other side. You want to know how your team is performing, how effective its leadership is. You want to know how considered are the positions taken by the other side, what are the "soft" spots in their approach (e.g., issues they do not discuss, or those they give telltale nonverbal reactions to).

Insight is built on observation skills constantly in use during negotiation or knowledge of the personalities and ideas of the other side, and on wide cultural knowledge of Japan and the Japanese. When dealing with people who are unexpressive, poker-faced, undemonstrative, the presence of someone insightful and knowledgeable about Japanese behavior and sensitive to their non-verbal behavior (like Midway of Calco, for instance) can be critically important.

Formulating Strategy: Given a negotiating team that is well balanced, options should develop as a matter of course, and "brainstorming" and other methods of facilitating the discovery of creative solutions can be used. The key to formulating strategies that may be highly effective lies in the extent to which you understand the real needs and interests of the other side. The offers or demands that people make do not necessarily represent the optimum or unique solution to the problem from their viewpoint. They are not necessarily more creative about solving their own problems than you are. A negotiator motivated in his choice of a position or price by the need to avoid showing a loss in his department on a particular project may well choose a figure that is merely a "round" number, e.g., $1,000. Suppose this will show a profit on his books of $400. Is it important to have exactly $400 book profit, at the expense of a conflict-ridden future relationship? Most unlikely. He himself may not know what profit figure will appear to be satisfactory, but if his need is appreciated by the other side, there may be room to negotiate a price that satisfies his need, and that of the other party through more rational ways than by just adhering to a "round" number. In short, understanding the needs of both sides is the only real basis for inventing alternatives that offer gain to both parties. Given, then, that this is a necessity, it will be clear that a principal focus of the preceding negotiating activity is to discover what these real needs are. And people are most likely to reveal their real needs and interests when they believe that the other side is trustworthy and fair.

Negotiating Options: The Strategic Negotiation Process assumes that by the time we get to negotiating options, all the "heavy" work of negotiation has been completed. There is good will between the sides, a high level of mutual understanding, and minimum bickering about offers and positions. It can now help, in reaching final agreement, to list the benefits and drawbacks of various options that have been proposed. The use of criteria (where possible) for objective assessments that can guide toward settling on a fair price, and so on, is often essential in international negotiations. Data on world prices, rather than someone's word on an acceptable price, take most of the conflict out of price debates. The question of concessions and their timing can arise for the first time at this point. Concessions as such (i.e., give-aways, premiums) are best given at the onset of agreement, to serve more as symbols of goodwill than as bargaining concessions.

THE STRATEGIC NEGOTIATION PROCESS: A SUMMARY STATEMENT

The Strategic Negotiation Process has been developed to meet an obvious need in negotiations with the Japanese, namely, how to reduce the problems that commonly occur, and, as we have seen, occur at every stage of negotiation. The term "strategic" here was chosen to indicate that effective negotiation demands a carefully planned, skillfully managed process of ongoing interaction with people we understand imperfectly, and with whom we can expect periodic difficulties, which must also be skillfully managed and overcome.

The first premise of SNP is that pre-negotiation planning, preparation, team development, and rehearsal are essential. Generally speaking, Westerners have much to learn as regards teamwork and team management, which are skills that their culture does not foster, and should therefore be learned from the Japanese.

When you are properly prepared, you are confident and able to make a comprehensive opening statement that, ideally, will sway the other side decisively to view the issue more as you do. The opening statement, properly done, is the reflection of a mature and considered standpoint and knowledge, and it will be seen as such. It can be a clear act of intellectual leadership (which Western culture does foster), especially when the negotiation issues are not entirely clear, when the other side is even more unsure than you are as to how or what to demand or concede, when objective criteria are lacking to make decisions beneficial to both sides. A two-sided, even-handed opening statement that is fair to both sides will be well accepted by the Japanese, and will keep the focus on broad issues, rather than on "penny ante" tactics or "nickel and dime" bargaining.

In other words, a broad opening statement has the effect of delaying bargaining with the Japanese (but this may not be true with other nationalities). If you are successful in this, there is a very good chance that you will secure a more grounded agreement, a better long-term relationship (if that is what you want), more long-term leverage on the Japanese side (who will have come to respect your sense of fairness and lack of horse-trader tactics), and a chance for effective bargaining close to reaching an agreement.

Along the way, SNP reminds us that there may be conflicts

and the need to exercise special skills. Conflicts, given the right team leader, are quickly handled—caucus, apology, expressing regret, are usually enough. Again, an effective team leader, rather than trying to handle everything alone, should call upon the special skills of his individual team members as the need arises. If team members don't have special skills, and don't get to use them, why are they on the team? If their only reason is to act as a cheer squad for the leader, that leader is not the man you need for handling complex negotiations with the Japanese.

Western negotiators need to be aware of the weakness of their negotiation teams, especially the tendency to lack integration and cohesion, and to be internally divisive. When this happens, experience suggests that either the team should be abandoned and just one competent, all-round negotiator be used; or, if a team is essential, a new team, one that is genuinely cooperative and organized behind one leader and spokesman, be selected.

BIBLIOGRAPHY

Acuff, F. L., and M. Villere. "Games Negotiators Play." *Business Horizons*, February 1976.

Asada, Fukuchi. *Kokusai torihiki keiyaku* (International Trade Contracts). Tokyo: Nunoi Shuppan, 1977.

Ballon, Robert J. *The Business Contract in Japan*. Sophia University Institute of Comparative Culture, Business Series No. 105 (1985).

Bartos, Otomar J. *Process and Outcome of Negotiations*. New York: Columbia University Press, 1985.

Bauer, R. A. "Accuracy of Perception in International Relations." *Teachers College Record* 64 (January 1960): 291–99.

Benedict, Ruth. *The Chrysanthemum and the Sword*. Rutland, Vt., and Tokyo: Charles E. Tuttle, 1976.

Bell, Coral. *Negotiation from Strength: A Study in the Politics of Power*. London: Chatto and Windus, 1962.

Blaker, Michael. *Nemawashi, kakimawashi, atomawashi: Nihon no kokusai kōshō taido no kenkyū* (Japanese International Negotiation Style). Tokyo: Simul Press, 1976.

———. *Japanese International Negotiation Style*. New York: Columbia University Press, 1977.

———. "Probe, Push and Panic: The Japanese Tactical Style in International Negotiations," in Robert Scalpino (ed.), *The Foreign Policy of Modern Japan*. Berkeley: University of California Press, 1977.

———. "The Japanese Tactical Negotiating Style Today," in Robert M. March (ed.), *Proceedings: Negotiating with Japanese Business and Government*. Brisbane: University of Queensland, August 1978.

Casse, P., and S. Deol. *Managing Intercultural Negotiations.* Washington, D.C.: SIETAR, 1985.

Coddington, A. *Theories of the Bargaining Process.* Chicago: Aldine Publishing, 1968.

Cohen, Bernard C. *The Political Process and Foreign Policy: The Making of the Japanese Peace Settlement.* Princeton, N.J.: Princeton University Press, 1957.

Cross, John G. *The Economics of Bargaining.* New York: Basic Books, 1970.

———. "Negotiation as a Learning Process," in William I. Zartman (ed.), *The Negotiation Process: Theories and Applications.* Beverly Hills: Sage Publications, 1977.

Davis, Paul A. *Long-Term Contracts with Japan.* Sydney: Australia Japan Trade Law Foundation, 1978.

Destler, I. M., H. Fukui, and H. Sato. *The Textile Wrangle.* Ithaca, N.Y.: Cornell University Press, 1979.

Deutsch, Mitchell F. *Doing Business with the Japanese.* New York: New American Library, 1974.

Dunn, Peter. "Are You a Good Negotiator?" *The National Times,* April 4–9, 1977: 47.

Ellsberg, Daniel. "Bargaining: Theory of the Reluctant Duelist," in Oran R. Young (ed.), *Bargaining: Formal Theories of Negotiation.* Chicago: University of Illinois Press, 1975.

Fayerweather, John, and Ashok Kapoor. "Simulated International Business Negotiations." *Journal of International Business Studies,* Spring 1972.

Fisher, Glen. *International Negotiation.* Chicago: Intercultural Press, 1980.

———. *The Cross-Cultural Dimension of Negotiations.* Chicago: Intercultural Press, 1980.

Fisher, Roger, and William Ury. *Getting to Yes: Negotiating Agreement Without Giving In.* Middlesex, England: Penguin Books, 1981.

Freed, Roy N. "American Lawyers in Japan." *The Japan Times,* April 5, 1987.

Gladwin, T., and I. Walter. *Multinationals Under Fire: Lessons in the Management of Conflict.* New York: Wiley, 1980.

Graham, John L. "Cross-Cultural Marketing Negotiations: A Laboratory Experiment." *Marketing Science,* 1985: 140–46.

Graham, John L., and Roy A. Herberger, Jr. "Negotiators Abroad Don't Shoot from the Hip." *Harvard Business Review,* July–August 1983.

Graham, John L. and Yoshihiro Sano. *Smart Bargaining: Doing Business with the Japanese*. Cambridge, Mass.: Ballinger Publishing Company, 1984.

Gray, Whitmore. "The Use and Non-Use of Contract Law in Japan: A Preliminary Study." *Law in Japan* 17 (1984).

Gulliver, P. J. *Disputes and Negotiations: A Cross-Cultural Perspective*. New York: Academic Press, 1971.

Hahn, Elliott J. "Negotiating with the Japanese: The American Method of Negotiating Contracts Does Not Fare Well in Japan." *California Lawyer* 2 (March 1982).

Hall, Edward T. *The Silent Language*. New York: Anchor Press, 1959.

———. "The Silent Language in Overseas Business." *Harvard Business Review*, May–June 1960.

Harnett, Donald L., and L. L. Cumings. *Bargaining Behavior*. Houston: Dame Publications, 1980.

Hoggart, Richard. *On Culture and Communication*. New York: Oxford University Press, 1972.

Horgan, E. F. "Canons of Negotiation: Some Principles for Licensing," in *Proceedings of the Licensing Executive Society Australia National Conference*, 1975.

Hoshino, Eiichi. "The Contemporary Contract." Translated by John O. Haley. *Law in Japan* 5, no. 1 (1972).

Ikle, Fred C. *How Nations Negotiate*. New York: Harper and Row, 1964.

Imai, Masaaki. *Sixteen Ways to Avoid Saying No: An Invitation to Experience Japanese Management from the Inside*. Tokyo: Toyota Motor Sales, 1981.

———. *Never Take Yes for an Answer: An Inside Look at Japanese Business for Foreign Businessmen*. Tokyo: Simul Press, 1982.

Jandt, F. E. *Win–Win Negotiating*. New York: Wiley, 1985.

Kaplan, E. J. "Perspectives on Government–Business Interaction in Japan," in Ashok Kapoor (ed.), *Asian Business*. Princeton, N.J.: Darwin Press, 1976.

Kapoor, Ashok. "International Business Negotiations: Characteristics and Planning Implications," in Ashok Kapoor (ed.), *Asian Business*. Princeton, N.J.: Darwin Press, 1976.

———. *Planning for International Business Negotiation*. Cambridge, Mass.: Ballinger, 1976.

Karrass, Chester L. *The Negotiation Game*. New York: Thomas Y. Crowell, 1970.

———. *Give and Take*. New York: Thomas Y. Crowell, 1974.

Kawaguchi, Etsuko, "The Japanese International Negotiation Style." Graduation thesis, International Christian University, Mitaka, Tokyo, 1986.

Kniveton, B., and B. Towers. *Training For Negotiation*. New Canaan, Ct.: Business Books, 1978.

Kumar, Rajesh. *Cognitive Foundations of Cross-Cultural Communication: A U.S. and Japanese Comparison*. NYU Business School, n.d. Mimeographed.

Lall, Arthur. *Modern International Negotiation*. New York: Columbia University Press, 1966.

————. *How Communist China Negotiates*. New York: Columbia University Press, 1968.

Lebra, T. S. *Japanese Patterns of Behavior*. Honolulu: University Press of Hawaii, 1976.

Lebra, T. S., and W. P. Lebra (eds.). *Japanese Culture and Behavior: Selected Readings*. Honolulu: University of Hawaii Press, 1974.

Lee, Sang W., and Gary Schwendiman (eds.). *Japanese Management: Cultural and Environmental Considerations*. New York: Praeger, 1982.

Lockhart, Charles. *Bargaining in International Conflicts*. New York: Columbia University Press, 1979.

MacDougall, Donald J. "Introduction to Negotiation Theory." *Law Institute Journal* 58 (December 1984).

March, Robert M. (ed.). "Communicating and Negotiating with the Japanese." University of Queensland Business Paper No. 8 (June 1977).

————. "Negotiation and Bargaining: A Review of the Literature." University of Queensland Business Paper No. 14 (March 1978).

———— (ed.). *Proceedings: Negotiating with Japanese Business and Government Symposium*. University of Queensland, August 1978.

————. "The Australia–Japan Sugar Negotiations." Australia–Japan Economic Relations Research Paper No. 56 (Canberra, March 1979).

————. "Melodrama in Japanese Negotiations." *Winds*, April 1982.

————. "How the Japanese Negotiate with Foreigners." *Marubeni World Report, April 1982*.

————. *"Yuben to kamoku no aida"* (Between Eloquence and Taciturnity). *Marubeni Monthly*, November 1982.

————. *Recent Japanese Negotiating Experience with Australian Companies*. Aoyama Gakuin University, July 1982. Xeroxed.

————. "Business Negotiation as Cross-Cultural Communication:

The Japanese–Western Case." *Cross Currents*, Spring 1982. (Also reprinted in *American Chamber of Commerce in Japan Journal, Speaking of Japan*, and *Tradepia International*.)

———. "Negotiating in the Land of Consensus." *The Imperial*, Fall 1983.

———. *"Kokuminsei karamu kōshō"* (Negotiation Involves National Character). *Seisansei Shimbun*, November 1983.

———. "The Silent Language of the Japanese." *Winds*, May 1984.

———. "East Meets West at the Negotiating Table." *Winds*, April 1985.

———. "How Well Do Your Staff Sell and Negotiate for You?" *American Chamber of Commerce in Japan Journal*, June 1985.

———. "The Nature of Negotiation and Japan's International Negotiation Style in Business." *Aoyama Journal of International Politics, Economics and Business*, November 1985.

———. "Sun Tzu, Chinese Military Strategist, and Japanese Business." *Winds*, January 1986.

———. *"Gaikokujin to no kōbai kōshō o jōzu ni susumeru ni wa"* (International Purchasing as Negotiation). *JMA Journal*, February 1986.

———. *"Yuganda kagami"* (The Distorted Mirror: Contemporary U.S.–Japan Negotiations). *JMA Journal*, October 1986.

———. "Negotiator's Casebook" (a 24-part series of Japanese/international negotiation case studies). *PHP Intersect*, January 1987 through December 1988.

———. *Nippon no gokai*. (Japan's Misunderstanding). Tokyo: Keizaikai Publishers, 1987.

———. *Nihonjin to kōshō suru hō* (How the Japanese Negotiate). Tokyo: PHP Publishers, 1987.

Marks, Bernard. *Australian–Japanese Business Transactions*. CCH Australia, 1978.

McCall, J. B., and M. B. Warrington. *Marketing by Agreement*. Chichester, N.Y.: Wiley, 1984.

McCreary, Don R. *Japanese–U.S. Business Negotiations*. New York: Praeger, 1986.

Menkel-Meadow, Carrie. "Legal Negotiation: A Study of Strategies in Search of a Theory." *American Bar Foundation Research Journal* 4 (1983).

Miller, Dudley L. "The Honorable Picnic: Doing Business in Japan." *Harvard Business Review*, Nov.–Dec. 1961.

Moran, R. T., and P. R. Harris. *Managing Cultural Synergy*. Houston: Gulf Publishing, 1981.

Moran, R. T. *Getting Your Yen's Worth*. Houston: Gulf Publishing, 1984.

Moore, C. A. (ed.). *The Japanese Mind*. Honolulu: University of Hawaii Press, 1967.

Morsbach, M. "Major Psychological Factors Influencing Japanese Interpersonal Relations," in N. Warren (ed.), *Studies in Cross-Cultural Psychology* 1. New York: Academic Press, 1980.

Morrison, W. F. *The Pre-Negotiation Planning Book*. New York: Wiley, 1985.

Mukō, Takao. *Kokusai keiyaku komyunikēshon* (Communication for International Commercial Contracts). Tokyo: Taishūkan, 1983.

Mushanokōji, Kinhide. *The Cultural Premises of Japan's Diplomacy*. Trilateral Commission Paper, 1975.

———. *The Silent Power: Japan's Identity and World Role*. Tokyo: Simul Press, 1976.

———. "The Strategies of Negotiation: An American–Japanese Comparison," in J. A. Laponce and Paul Smoker (eds.), *Experimentation and Simulation in Political Science*. Toronto: University of Toronto Press, 1972.

Nakamura, Hajime. *Ways of Thinking of Eastern Peoples: India, China, Tibet and Japan*. Honolulu: University of Hawaii Press, 1964.

Nakamura, Hideo. *Eibun keiyakusho sakusei no kīpointo* (Keypoints in Preparing English-Language Contracts). Tokyo: Commercial Law Center, 1985.

Nakane, Chie. *Japanese Society*. Middlesex, England: Penguin Books, 1973.

New Yorker Magazine. "Annals of Law: The Betamax Case I," April 6, 1987.

Nierenberg, Gerard I. *The Art of Negotiating*. New York: Hawthorn Books, 1968.

———. *Fundamentals of Negotiation*. New York: Hawthorn Books, 1973.

Nishikata, Masumi. "Kare o shiraba hyakusen ayau karazu" (Know Your Enemy, and Be Fearless in a Hundred Battles). *Business View*, April 1980: 14–21.

Norbury, Paul, and Geoffrey Bownas (eds.). *Business in Japan: A Guide to Japanese Business Practice and Procedure*. Boulder, Colorado: Westview Press, 1980.

Okonogi, Keigo. "The Ajase Complex of the Japanese (2)." *Japan Echo* VI, no. 1 (1979): 104–18.

Pascale, Richard T., and A. G. Athos. *The Art of Japanese Management: Applications for American Executives*. New York: Simon and Schuster, 1981.

Pruitt, D. G. *Negotiation Behavior*. New York: Academic Press, 1981.

Pye, Lucian. *Chinese Commercial Negotiating Style*. Cambridge, Mass.: Oelgeschlager, Gunn and Hain, 1982.

Raiffa, Howard. *The Art and Science of Negotiation*. Cambridge, Mass.: Harvard University Press, 1982.

Rapoport, A. *Fights, Games and Debates*. Ann Arbor: University of Michigan Press, 1960.

Ratiu, Indrei. "Thinking Internationally: A Comparison of How International Executives Learn." *International Studies of Management and Organization* XIII, no. 1–2 (1983): 139–50.

Reardon, K. K. *Persuasion: Theory and Context*. Beverly Hills: Sage Publishing, 1980.

Ruben, Brent D., and Daniel J. Kealey. "Behavioral Assessment of Communication Competencies and the Prediction of Cross-Cultural Adaptation." *International Journal of Intercultural Relations* 3 (1979).

Rubin, J. Z., and B. R. Brown. *The Social Psychology of Bargaining and Negotiation*. New York: Academic Press, 1975.

Sawada, J. T. *Subsequent Conduct and Supervening Events*. Tokyo: University of Tokyo Press, 1968.

Schelling, Thomas C. *The Strategy of Conflict*. Cambridge, Mass.: Harvard University Press, 1960.

————. "An Essay on Bargaining," in Oran R. Young (ed.), *Bargaining*. Chicago: University of Illinois Press, 1975.

Spector, Bertram I. "Negotiation as a Psychological Process," in William I. Zartman (ed.), *The Negotiation Process: Theories and Applications*. Beverly Hills: Sage Publications, 1977.

Stening, Bruce W. "Problems in Cross-Cultural Contact: A Literature Review 2." *International Journal of Intercultural Relations* 3 (1979).

Stewart, Edward C. P. "Western Dreams and Japanese Decisions: The Cross-Cultural Communication Gap." *Speaking of Japan* 7 (April 1986).

Swingle, P. (ed.). *The Structure of Conflict*. New York: Academic Press, 1970.

Taylor, Jared. *Shadows of the Rising Sun: A Critical View of the "Japanese Miracle."* Rutland, Vt., and Tokyo: Charles E. Tuttle, 1983.

Tedeschi, J. T., B. R. Schleuker, and T. V. Bonoma. *Conflict, Power* and *Games*. Chicago: Aldine, 1972.

Tokuyama, Jirō. "The Japanese Notion of Law: An Introduction to Flexibility and Indefinitude," in Ashok Kapoor (ed.), *Asian Business*. Princeton, N.J.: Darwin Press, 1976.

Tung, Rosalie L. "How To Negotiate with the Japanese." *California Management Review*, Summer 1984.

——. *Business Negotiations with the Japanese*. Lexington, Mass.: Lexington Books, 1984.

Van de Velde, James. "The Influence of Culture on Japanese–American Negotiations." *Fletcher Forum* 7 (Summer 1983).

Van Zandt, Howard F. "How to Negotiate in Japan." *Harvard Business Review*, Nov.–Dec. 1970.

Weiss, Stephen E. "Negotiating with Foreign Businessmen: An Introduction for Americans with Propositions on Six Cultures." Working paper, Graduate School of Business Administration. New York: New York University, 1984.

——. "Greeting the GM–Toyota Joint Venture: A Case in Complex Negotiation." *Columbia Journal of World Business* 22, no. 2 (1987).

Weisz, J. R., et al. "Standing Out and Standing In: The Psychology of Control in America and Japan." *American Psychologist*, September 1984: 954–69.

Winkler, John, *Pricing for Results*. New York: Facts on File Publications, 1984.

Young, Oran R. (ed.). *Bargaining: Formal Theories of Negotiation*. Chicago: University of Illinois Press, 1975.

Zaroom, Anthony E. "*Amerikajin bengoshi no mita Nihon no hō bunka: Senmonka no adobaisu*" (Japanese Law from an American Lawyer's Perspective: Some Advice). *Shosai no Mado* 2 (1984).

——. "*Soshō girai*" (Disliking Litigation). *Shosai no Mado* 4 (1984).

——. "*Tate shakai*" (The Vertical Society). *Shosai no Mado* 7 (1984).

——. "*Giri ninjō*" (Human Relations). *Shosai no Mado* 9 (1984).

Zartman, William I. (ed.). *The Negotiation Process: Theories and Applications*. Beverly Hills: Sage Publications, 1977.

Zartman, William I., and Maureen R. Berman. *The Practical Negotiator*. New Haven, Ct.: Yale University Press, 1982.

Zimmerman, Mark. *How To Do Business with the Japanese*. New York: Random House, 1985.

INDEX

account managers, 65–80, 134
administrative guidance, 40
agendas, 62, 87, 95, 96, 134, 162, 178
Akutagawa, Ryūnosuke, 149
amae (dependency), 134
ambiguity, use of, 16
American Chamber of Commerce in Japan Journal, 77
analytical ability, as key skill, 178
aristocratic values, 17
assertive strategies. *See* strategies, assertive.
avoidance of self-praise, 32
avoidance strategies. *See* strategies, avoidance.

bargaining, 15, 16, 70, 72, 84, 154
bargaining stage, of negotiation, 161, 166–67
baseball. *See* Egawa baseball dispute.
behavior, Japanese, 17
behind-the-scenes activity, 138
Betamax lawsuit, 119–23
Blaker, Michael, 25, 129, 130, 138
body language, 73; *see also* nonverbal expression.
bulldozing, 138

bureaucratic attitude to foreigners, 40
business manners, 78
buyer-seller relationship, 113

Calco case study, 69–75, 79, 181
case studies. *See* Calco; Hitoba; Japan–Australia sugar dispute; Mansha–Mannheim; Neuerbach; Nippon Texacom; Toyomitsu; Toyosan; "two broadcasting organizations"; Warner–Natsuyama.
CBS, 120
"changed circumstances" (*jijō henkō*), 112, 114, 116, 118, 129
commercial ostracism, 107
communication, as key skill, 179–80
communication skills, 45, 155–56
complication stage, of negotiation, 161, 167–68
comprehensive opening statement, 94, 160, 173–74, 183
compromise, 128
concealing the top man, strategy of. *See* strategies.
concessions, 46, 54, 63, 73, 74, 77, 101, 130, 137, 154, 160, 163, 167, 168, 182

conflict, 89, 184; quick resolution of, 175, 177; roots of, 83–88
conscience, in Japan, 27
consensus, 9, 76, 77, 130, 131, 132, 154, 159, 163
contracts, 17, 32, 54, 66, 70, 74, 78, 86, 89, 97, 98, 99, 100, 101, 102, 129; Japanese attitudes to, 111–23
counteroffers, 85
cross-cultural minsunderstandings, 42
cross-cultural negotiation, 7, 35, 42, 63, 83, 169

decision-makers, 50, 86, 87, 104, 136, 137, 159
deferrals, 141
delayed bargaining, 174–75
difficulties of negotiating in English, 9
diplomatic negotiating style, 25
discounts, 74
disguising feelings, 32
Doyle Dane Bernbach, 120, 121
"economic animals," 17

Egawa baseball dispute (1978), 112–13
exercise of power, 21
extroverts, 110
eyes, in nonverbal expression, 146–48

face, in nonverbal expression, 145–46
"face-saving," 74
face-to-face communication/negotiation, 88, 93, 110, 163
Fair Trade Commission (FTC), 39,40
feedback, 87
flattery, 145
frankness, 88, 96
Freed, Roy N., 119
friendship relationship, 20
frustration, 109

FTC, 41
Fukuda Cabinet, 101

gimu (obligation to society), 128
giri (obligation to parents and seniors), 128
give-and-take, 28, 29, 130
"go-betweens." See middlemen.
Graham, John L., and Yoshihiro Sano, 133, 135, 139, 140
group basis, for Japanese decisions, 67
group synchrony, 151–52

hands, in nonverbal expression, 148–49
hierarchical society, 16, 21
Hitoba case study, 60–64
honne, 141–42

IBM, 31
iiau, 84
imitation, of the other side's style, 57, 60, 61, 63–64
impassivity, Japanese, 143
indebtedness, 28
indifference to time, 64, 175
indirect suggestion, 21
indirectness, 32
industrial espionage, 30, 31
information-gathering, 30, 32
information-orientation, Japanese, 134–35
inscrutability, Japanese, 152
insight, as key skill, 181
insurance, 37, 38
international managers, 46, 170–72
international negotiation problems, resolving, 169–84
interpersonal relationships, 35
interpreters, 53, 58, 83, 93, 94, 104
intimidation, 87
introverts, 110
intuitive knowledge/understanding, 21, 59, 156

Japan–Australia Long-Term Sugar Agreement, 98
Japan–Australia sugar dispute, 26, 54, 97–107, 108, 112, 113, 129, 134, 138
Japanese domestic negotiation style, 32; *see also* negotiation, Japanese style.
joint ventures, 11, 36, 37, 38, 39, 166

Kawaguchi, Etsuko, 136
key skills, in Strategic Negotiation Process, 169–70, 177–82
kikkake, 22, 24
kōshō, 84

lack of hurry, 154
language, problems of, 41, 84, 85, 86
law offices in Japan, 117
lawyers, 116–19; foreign, 118
life insurance, 38
London Commodities Market, 70
long-term contracts (LTCs), 97, 98–102, 105–6
long-term customers, 74
long-term relationships/ties, 36, 56, 66, 75, 89, 183

management skills, importance of, 35, 42
managers, 39, 42, 46, 47, 51, 53, 65, 69, 70, 75, 78, 79, 80, 170, 171–72
Mansha–Mannheim case study, 36–42, 46, 51, 57
market fluctuations, 78
mass media, 102–3
MCA, 119, 120, 121
means to influence others, Japanese, 17
melodrama, 24, 25, 115
middlemen/"go betweens," use of, 16, 92, 135–36
minimum royalty, 89, 90, 91, 92
Ministry of Agriculture, Forestry and Fisheries (MAF), 99, 100, 101, 103
Ministry of Finance (MOF), 37, 39, 40, 41
Ministry of Foreign Affairs, 103, 104
Ministry of Health and Welfare, 31
Ministry of International Trade and Industry (MITI), 39, 40, 103, 109
misunderstandings, 39, 68, 57, 83, 86, 104, 156, 166, 180
Mitsubishi trading company, 99
Mitsui trading company, 99
Morsbach, M., 130
Morita, Akio, 119–23
Morrison, W. F., 162
mouth, in nonverbal expression, 148
mutual interest, 35

naniwabushi, 22–25, 26, 32, 107, 115, 127, 129, 134
national pride, Japanese, 54, 157
NBC, 120
negotiating options, 182
negotiation, game-type, 34–35, 55, 83; psychology of Japanese, 21–33; tactical-type, 34–35, 83
negotiation strategies, Japanese, 127–52
negotiation style, Japanese, 8–10, 16, 31–32, 63–64, 127–52, 153–57, 162–62, 166–68; American/Western, 8–10, 16, 63–64, 164–65, 166–68
negotiation teams, importance of unity of, 68
negotiation training programs, 7–10, 84, 109–10, 161–62
nemawashi, 27, 31, 178
Neuerbach case study, 65–69, 79, 153
Nihon Keizai Shimbun, 99, 103
Nippon Steel, 68, 138
Nippon Texacom case study, 32, 51–55, 134, 157
normative strategies. *See* strategies, normative.

nonverbal behavior/expression, 95, 96, 141–52
nonverbal feedback/signs, 59, 87

obligation, 128–29
obliqueness, 32
"offer price," 71, 72
Okonogi, Keigo, 25, 28, 29, 157
on (obligation incurred), 28, 128
opening stage, of negotiation, 161, 164–66
opening statement. *See* comprehensive opening statement.
ostracism, as technique of social control, 29; *see also* commercial ostracism.

padded offers, 135
patience, 17, 108
permissible commercial behavior, 109
persistence, 130
personal connections (*kone*), 28
personal relationships/ties, 19, 66
politeness, 128, 157
post-agreement problems, 129
postponements, 141
posture, Japanese, 150
pre-giving, 27–28, 128–29
pre-negotiation, 95, 153, 161, 162–64, 183
presentations, 95
professional managers, 79, 80
psychology, Japanese, 25

rational strategies. *See* strategies, rational.
Ratiu, Indrei, 170
recess, 73
reciprocity, 134
re-negotiation, 133
representative offices in Japan, importance of, 78
role plays, 7, 10

secretiveness, 86
seme, 22, 24
sempai–kohai (elder–younger) relationship, 29, 139
service, 18, 20, 21, 137
shirankao, 145, 147
short-term profits, 75
silence, use of, 140–41
solving problems, 128
Sonam, 120, 121
Sony Corporation, 119–23
speaking ambiguously, 16
stereotypes, 79, 83, 85, 159, 160
Strategic Negotiation Process (SNP), 12, 172–84
strategic options, 16
strategies: assertive, 138–40; avoidance, 140–41; concealing the top man, 31, 50, 136–37; normative, 127–31; rational, 131–38; *see also* *naniwabushi*.
strengths, of Japanese as negotiators, 153–55
Sugar Board, of Australia, 104
sugar dispute. *See* Japan–Australia sugar dispute.
Sullivan Mission, 100
Sun-tzu, 29–30, 31
supermarkets, 18
suppressing feelings, 32
susceptibility to sad stories, Japanese, 24

tactical behavior, 55
tactical blocking, 132
tactical questioning, 139
tactics, 86, 106, 107; *see also* strategies.
"target price", 72
tariff barriers, 99
tatemae, 142–44, 146, 148, 151
team development/organization, 129, 131–33, 155–54, 155, 162, 163, 172–73, 177, 180, 183, 184
teamwork, 87, 131, 153, 173

Toyomitsu case study, 43–47, 51, 54
Toyosan case study, 47–50, 51, 138
trust, 17, 66, 128, 133
"two broadcasting organizations" case study, 57–60, 84, 156

United Kingdom, 47, 48
Universal Pictures, 119–23
urei, 22

verbal aggression, 84, 85
verbal contracts, 32
verbosity, 88
victim mentality (*higaisha ishiki*), 26

virtue, as model, 21
voluntary restraint, 49

Warner–Natsuyama case study, 32, 88–97, 108, 136, 138, 156, 157, 174, 175–76, 177
weaknesses, of Japanese as negotiators, 155–57
Western negotiation teams, 50, 131, 136

Yokohama, 101, 106

Zaroom, Anthony E., 76, 77